"I am very happy these cases are being highlighted, as there are many stories in which the truth has been hidden. These are enigmas that continue to haunt many Malaysians."

Kuan Chee Heng
Founder of Community Policing Malaysia

"The cases chosen are very interesting. Fairness, unbiased investigation and speed without compromising professionalism is the essence of police work. Just as justice must be seen to be served, the human rights of the victims and the perpetrators' families must also be protected. The authors have done well on a challenging subject."

A. Thaiveegan
Commissioner of Police (retired)

D1528066

MALAYSIAN MURDERS AND MYSTERIES

A century of shocking cases
that gripped the nation

Martin Vengadesan AND Andrew Sagayam

Marshall Cavendish
Editions

© 2020 Marshall Cavendish International (Asia) Pte Ltd
Text © Martin Vengadesan & Andrew Sagayam

Published by Marshall Cavendish Editions
An imprint of Marshall Cavendish International

Reprinted 2020

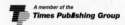

A member of the
Times Publishing Group

Other Marshall Cavendish Offices:
Marshall Cavendish Corporation, 99 White Plains Road, Tarrytown NY 10591-9001,
USA • Marshall Cavendish International (Thailand) Co Ltd, 253 Asoke, 12th Flr,
Sukhumvit 21 Road, Klongtoey Nua, Wattana, Bangkok 10110, Thailand • Marshall
Cavendish (Malaysia) Sdn Bhd, Times Subang, Lot 46, Subang Hi-Tech Industrial Park,
Batu Tiga, 40000 Shah Alam, Selangor Darul Ehsan, Malaysia.

Marshall Cavendish is a registered trademark of Times Publishing Limited

National Library Board, Singapore Cataloguing in Publication Data

Names: Vengadesan, Martin. | Sagayam, Andrew.
Title: Malaysian murders and mysteries : a century of shocking cases that gripped the
nation / Martin Vengadesan and Andrew Sagayam.
Description: Singapore : Marshall Cavendish Editions, [2019]
Identifiers: OCN 1119530255 | ISBN 978-981-48-6855-6 (paperback) |
Subjects: LCSH: Crime--Malaysia. | Murder--Malaysia. | True crime stories--Malaysia.
Classification: DDC 364.9595--dc23

Printed in Singapore

Dedicated to all victims of violent crimes in Malaysia,
especially victims of crimes which remain unsolved.
To the family members who have suffered alongside them.
To those who have fought for justice, and also to
those punished for crimes they did not commit.

A special thank you to
the late Karpal Singh and
the late Professor Khoo Kay Kim
who gave their time to this book.

CONTENTS

INTRODUCTION

Every country has its own salacious scandals, gruesome crimes and unsolved mysteries. The lore of the Malay Peninsula is rich with stories of murder and intrigue surrounding such mythical figures as Hang Tuah and Mahsuri.

Modern Malaysia is no different. Over the past century, there have been cases that have gripped the attention of the entire nation only to become vague memories as time passes.

These crimes vary in nature and detail. In some instances the perpetrators have been caught and punished, while others remain unresolved. What most of them have in common is that they were real-life dramas played out through the media and thus carried into every home in the country. Ordinary Malaysians have been morbidly drawn to the darkness that can exist in the hearts of the worst and, sometimes, the best of us.

Motives varied from heated crimes of passion to cynical executions for profit or even simple cruelty. The criminals were sadistic, cool, twisted, ingenious and sometimes even credited with supernatural powers!

It has to be said that in compiling this book, we came across cases which are still rather 'sensitive' (and we use that term in its all-encompassing, peculiarly Malaysian glory).

We are referring not just to ongoing trials such as the 1MDB legal cases and the Kevin Morais murder proceedings under which comment might be sub judice, but rather to situations in which prominent personalities who were implicated but not charged are still in a position to suppress the truth. Thus, one may find omissions that prevent this work from being the free-flowing exposé it should be.

Still, we were fortunate enough to be able to talk to some of the most eminent historians and criminal lawyers, crime reporters and police officers in the country, and they were able to breathe new life into some of the cases and shed new light on these notorious events. We hasten to add that many of these cases deserve a single book unto themselves and what we are providing here is but a summary with some fresh insights, rather than an in-depth look into any specific crime.

We go as far back as 1875, beginning with colonial-era intrigues that remain unresolved to this day and investigate over a century of Malaysian murders and mysteries.

1

THE RESIDENT
IN THE OUTHOUSE

Date : November 2, 1875
Crime : James Birch is murdered while in the bath

Details: In November 1874, James Wheeler Woodford Birch was appointed the first British Resident to the princely state of Perak in accordance with the Pangkor Treaty signed earlier that year. A year later, he was viciously murdered by a local chieftain and his followers. Explanations over the motives may differ, but the fact remains that JWW Birch was executed for his very presence in the heart of Malaya.

Speaking in 2012, the late Professor Emeritus Dr Khoo Kay Kim, a long-time professor of history at the University of Malaya, set the scene: "After the British came into Malaya, they gradually took control of the administration. However, sovereignty was still technically with the rulers,

Professor Khoo Kay Kim. *The Star* file image (courtesy of Star Media Group).

the sultans. In many states, it was the local headmen who lost their authority and they rose against the British."

At the time, the state of Perak was in chaos. Rival claimants disputed the succession to the throne after the death of Sultan Ali Inayat Shah in 1871. The rightful heir, Raja Abdullah, did not assume the leadership which had fallen into the hands of Raja Ismail instead. It was mainly for this reason that Raja Abdullah signed the Pangkor Treaty. That treaty forced Raja Ismail to step down, but also meant that the new Sultan Abdullah was reliant on British support.

Unfortunately, Birch proved a headstrong leader who managed to anger not just supporters of the de-throned Raja Ismail, but Sultan Abdullah as well. He was widely perceived as having no regard for local customs and beliefs.

Matters came to a head when Birch decided to impose a set of regulations on the locals. The events were to be described decades later by Birch's successor Sir Frank Swettenham in his book *Malay Sketches*, which was published in 1895.

According to Swettenham, a local chieftain Maharaja Lela was in power at Pasir Salak at the time. When he met Sultan Abdullah, Maharaja Lela informed him in no uncertain terms that he was not going to submit to any form of authority that Birch would impose upon him. Sultan Abdullah did not oppose his decision.

Thus it was that when Birch sailed into Pasir Salak and docked his boat near the bath house of a Chinese jeweller, he was sailing into a situation of great tension. For a start his Sikh guards were reluctant to enter a potentially explosive situation and his interpreter, in particular, was aware that local sentiment was very much against him.

Despite the presence of a large number of angry villagers led by Maharaja Lela's father-in-law Pandak Indut and a fanatical follower named Siputum, Birch ordered that the regulations be posted all over Pasir Salak. He then went into the floating bath house with an armed Sikh guard watching the entrance.

This was simply not enough. His interpreter and Pandak Indut immediately got into a dispute over one of the printed regulation papers, and the former was fatally speared. The Sikh guard charged with guarding the bath house fled. As the scuffle boiled over into a full-fledged melee, Birch popped his head out of the bath house.

Siputum slashed his head with a machete and Birch's body sank into the waters. Birch's entourage tried to flee, but three others (the boatman, the interpreter and another Sikh Guard) lost their lives.

Khoo said: "In this instance, Maharaja Lela was angered by Birch's actions, which were impinging on his livelihood and diminishing his authority, and he killed him for it. Some will say he was a nationalist. The British might try to portray Birch as a well-meaning reformer."

Certainly there are varying reasons ascribed to this particular clash of wills. While Maharaja Lela is now considered a nationalist hero, he is widely believed to have been a slave trader. At the time, certain segments of Malay society used the Orang Asli people as slaves and Maharaja Lela was benefitting from this lucrative business. This was quite possibly abhorrent to Birch. On the other hand, Birch could just have been an arrogant white man determined to stamp his authority on a village chieftain whose power he underestimated.

The death of Birch had a significant impact on the political landscape of Perak. After a brief period of 'power', Maharaja Lela was defeated militarily and apprehended. Over the course of a week in December 1876, he and his cohorts were tried for murder in the new administrative capital of Taiping. Swettenham himself was one of the prosecuting officers for Maharaja Lela, Pandak Indut and five others. Maharaja Lela, Pandak Indut and one other were sentenced to death and the hanging was carried out on January 20, 1877.

Ultimately, both Sultan Abdullah and his predecessor, Sultan Ismail, were censured and banished from the state (the former sent to the Seychelles). Ironically, this left another of Sultan Abdullah's rivals, Sultan Yusuf, to assume the throne.

VERDICT This killing was both political and personal even though there is a possibility that Maharaja Lela never actually met Birch himself personally. Birch's murderers were tried, sentenced and executed but the impact of the incident was felt for decades afterwards.

2

THE MURDER AT VICTORIA INSTITUTION

Date : April 23, 1911

Crime : A British engineer is shot dead on the grounds of one of Malaya's foremost schools

Details: This case is a colonial-era scandal that played itself out on the grounds of Victoria Institution (VI). At that time, Malaya was very much under colonial thumb and while the locals may or may not have comported themselves well, their colonial 'masters' were expected to behave in a manner that befitted their status as superiors.

Imagine the scandal when engineer William Crozier Steward was found dead on the verandah of the headmaster's bungalow at Victoria Institution, what more when the acting headmaster, William Proudlock, was out to dinner leaving only his young wife, Ethel, at home. It was practically a scene out of an Agatha Christie crime novel ... given that Christie published her first book *The*

Mysterious Affair At Styles a few years after, perhaps this murder served to inspire!

Proudlock was well regarded in his profession. A protege of headmaster Bennett Shaw, he was seen as a key asset to help cope with the demands of the fast-growing school. In 1907, Proudlock married Ethel Charter at St Mary's Anglican Church, beside what is now Dataran Merdeka.

William Proudlock was appointed the acting headmaster of VI during one of Shaw's trips back to the UK and moved into the headmaster's bungalow with Ethel and their three-year-old daughter. However, this idyllic scene was shattered when on the night of April 23, 1911, the visiting Steward was found shot dead on the verandah of said bungalow.

Steward, formerly the manager of Salak South Tin Mine, had arrived at the bungalow by rickshaw and asked the boy who pulled the rickshaw to wait for him. A short while later, the boy heard shots and saw Steward fall to the ground. More shockingly, he was followed by Ethel Proudlock, who emptied the remaining bullets into his body!

Far from the stiff upper lip required of members of the British colonial machine, it appeared as if the shooting was engendered by steamy passion more commonly associated with the 'savages' the Empire was trying to civilise. Within a few weeks of the incident, Ethel Proudlock was in the dock, claiming that Steward had approached her aggressively and she had had no choice but to shoot him in self-defence.

On the other hand, rumours were rife that Ethel had fallen in love with the dashing Steward and engaged in an affair with him behind the back of her work-obsessed husband. On that fateful night, Steward had come to call it off and say goodbye only to be greeted and dispatched by a woman scorned.

Ethel's claims did not resonate with the judge and he sentenced her to death. Kuala Lumpur's scandalised colonial society took stock of the event, and tried to prevent it from damaging its own image, while Ethel spent five months in KL's iconic Pudu Jail. Eventually, she was released thanks to the clemency of then Sultan of Selangor Sultan Sir Alaeddin Sulaiman Shah.

The Proudlocks immediately fled Malaya and began a roving life that would see them move first to the UK and then Canada. At some point during World War I (1914-1918), Ethel Proudlock moved to the USA with her daughter, while William continued on his own, working as a teacher and eventually settling in Argentina, where he gave many years of service to St George's School in Quilmes.

He died in Argentina in 1958, and Ethel passed away in the USA in the 1970s. However, by that time the tale of this scandalous crime had been told and retold in many incarnations. Legendary author Somerset Maugham reworked it into a short story called *The Letter*, which itself was transformed by a fair number of cinematic adaptations. The most famous was a film noir starring Bette Davis and needless to say, the facts were sufficiently distorted that the story had been transplanted, gallingly enough, to Singapore!

The Proudlock case was later given a thorough examination by author Eric Lawlor, whose 1999 publication

Murder on the Verandah: Love and Betrayal in British Malaya revived interest in the case. Unlike a typical Hercule Poirot novel, however, there is no neat little bow with which to tie this case up.

VERDICT Ethel Proudlock was found guilty of Steward's murder and sentenced to death, but upon appeal was released after just five months. There can be little doubt that this was a steamy crime of passion.

3

TOK JANGGUT STRIKES A BLOW

Date : April 29, 1915
Crime : A policeman is stabbed to death in a fight with a Malay chieftain

Details: At first glance, this seemed like a small provincial crime. In the sleepy town of Pasir Puteh, Sergeant Che Wan Sulaiman was stabbed to death by Haji Hassan Mat Munas. The latter was a religious teacher better known by the moniker Tok Janggut, on account of his prodigious facial hair. However, details of the crime and the punishment show that the killing was part of a larger struggle — that of a period of Malay history when its people found themselves subjugated.

At the time, Tok Janggut was going to be detained for failing to pay his taxes. However, a dispute over his reluctance to walk in front of his arresting officer led to a scuffle during which Tok Janggut fatally stabbed Sergeant Che Wan with his keris.

Professor Khoo explained: "Tok Janggut certainly felt he was going against the British but by law he was going against royalty, in this case Sultan Muhammad IV of Kelantan. The British moved quickly to brand him a traitor. At that time Tok Janggut had his followers but he might not necessarily have seen himself as an independence fighter. It was only later that politicians sought to label him as such.

"What happened certainly has its parallels in the 1875 murder of Birch. In that instance, Maharaja Lela was angered by Birch's actions which were impinging on his livelihood and diminishing his authority, and he killed him for it.

"In this case, Tok Janggut killed a fellow Malay, yes, but one from Singapore. At that point Malays were much more aware of territorial and clannish affiliations. It was significant to them which region of Indonesia they were descended from. Furthermore, he viewed the Malay he killed as an agent of the British."

In the aftermath of the murder, Tok Janggut gathered his followers and marched on Pasir Puteh itself. He briefly took over the administration with one Engku Besar Jeram, who had also suffered a diminished role under the new regime. Within days, however, Tok Janggut was defeated in battle and executed, his corpse exhibited prominently as a deterrent against further rebellion.

Khoo said: "The British tended to act in haste. They didn't understand that local people didn't understand their laws and that traditions were more important to them. They could be obedient to a ruler but resented outsiders.

"They hung him upside down. That was how the British instilled fear. They brought in soldiers from outside and people like Tok Janggut had local support in terms of sentiment but they were not strong enough or organised enough to challenge the British."

It was perhaps significant that just two months earlier the Mutiny of the 5th Native Light Infantry had broken out in Singapore. This mutiny, which began on February 15, 1915, resulted from the rebellion of conscripted Indian soldiers against the British. Mainly Indian Muslims, the soldiers objected to the fact that as components of the British war machine, they were expected to fight against Turkey as part of Britain's commitments in the First World War. The mutiny resulted in the deaths of 47 British soldiers and local civilians before it was brutally suppressed.

Khoo said: "The Singapore mutiny had a great effect on British attitude towards Islam. The mutiny was a result of the British being at war with the Ottoman Empire, as Turkey then was called. The Turks had joined in World War I on Germany's side. Turkey, at the time, was regarded by Muslims as the caliphate. And so, the British soldiers in Singapore, mainly Indian Muslims, decided to mount a revolt. This made the British very wary of their hold on the Malay peninsula and explains why they acted so ruthlessly to crush Tok Janggut."

Distinguished Professor Dr Shamsul Amri Baharuddin concurs. "What happened with Tok Janggut is certainly not an isolated case of a man acting alone. It is part of

Professor Shamsul Amri Baharuddin (courtesy of Institute of Ethnic Studies, UKM).

a larger wave of Malay opposition to the British, either through nationalism or religious sentiments or both. There is the little-known Terengganu uprising of 1928 in which protesters occupied a police station in opposition to the British, who had 11 of them killed. You look at Datuk Bahaman and Mat Kilau (who led the Pahang Rebellion of 1891–1895).

"It is clear that they represent a group of people unwilling to live under the British. From a strictly legal point of view, it may be that a murder was committed, but under different circumstances, history might judge the Tok Janggut case to be a rebellion."

There is an interesting aside to this story. In 1970, a man claimed to be Mat Kilau, aged 122 no less! A committee was formed to investigate his claim, and on August 6, 1970, Pahang Chief Minister Yahya Mohd Seh declared that this man was indeed the legendary warrior. Sadly, he died within four days of the proclamation!

VERDICT Tok Janggut was clearly guilty of the murder of Sergeant Che Wan. While his cause may have been just, the officer did not deserve such an undignified end. Then again, neither did Tok Janggut.

4

THE BATANG KALI MASSACRE

Date : December 12, 1948
Crime : British troops kill 24 unarmed villagers in the early
           months of the Malayan Emergency

Details: In 1948, the Malayan Emergency was just hotting up. The country may have become weary of four brutal years of Japanese occupation, but the brief post-war dominance of the Communist Party of Malaya (CPM) was clearly at odds with the desire of the British authorities to reclaim a territory whose raw materials would be seized and exploited to help the United Kingdom rebuild itself.

By 1948, the conflict between the communists and the British had erupted into an 'undeclared war' that would be waged from 1948 to 1960. British forces sought to subdue the communists, who had gained a degree of popularity for their resistance towards the Japanese. It didn't help that in China, Mao's Communist Party was on the verge of defeating the Kuomintang.

It was against this backdrop that the 7th Platoon of G Company of the second battalion of Scots Guards unit of the British Army belied its gallant reputation. Under the leadership of Sergeant Charles Douglas, the guards surrounded a rubber estate near Batang Kali, Selangor. Looking for communist guerrillas who weaved in and out of the local population, they shot and killed 24 ethnic Chinese villagers before razing the village.

The next day, local daily *The Straits Times* carried a report stating 'Scots Guards and Police were today reported to have shot dead 25 out of 26 bandits during a wide-scale operation in North Selangor'. It called the killings 'the biggest success as yet achieved in one operation in Malaya since the Emergency began'.

It was a bold-faced lie. The guards may have been acting on false information or may have panicked but many innocent people were killed. Worse still, the incident was hushed up, only surviving as whispers through time.

There were, however, a few survivors. One man had fainted and was presumed dead, while some women and children lived to tell the tale. According to them, the Scots Guards had separated the men to be interrogated before it turned into a rampage of indiscriminate shooting.

"At the time we didn't hear much," recalled Professor Khoo. "We just heard some rumours. I would not call it an everyday occurrence, but no doubt it happened at a time when there was a lot of tension. What happened at Batang Kali was due in part to the complexity of society. It is almost unavoidable in times of conflict and hatred between ethnic and territorial groups. I see it as a conflict of cultures.

"From what I understand, they were innocent men. But the Chinese may well have reacted in a peculiar way that would have seemed suspicious to the British, who were paranoid and ignorant of local ways. The British always had problems with the Chinese community. That is why the Governor Sir Shenton Thomas tried to come up with a programme to anglicise the Chinese, but they were not easily controlled.

"At that point, the Chinese were under the influence of the leftists and the secret societies. They were themselves enemies within the community and in some ways it mirrored the conflict in China between the Kuomintang and the Communist Party."

Professor Shamsul laments the tragic loss of life. "At the time the British would have had their own people on the ground. But informers can make the biggest mistakes, sometimes even on purpose. It is possible that the informer didn't like these people. In this case, it is likely that the British acted on wrong information. It is difficult to be an informer/undercover agent because both sides will crucify you. In fact at that very time, the leader of the communists Loi Tak was a triple agent, a Vietnamese who worked for the Japanese and the British while leading the CPM!

"The conditions of war generate different dynamics, which we can still see today in Afghanistan and Iraq where there are many vendetta killings and economic killings done under falsified circumstances."

Leon Comber played a critical role in the formative years of our police force's Special Branch and spent many years countering the communist insurgency. The author of *Malaya's Secret Police, 1945-1960: The Role of the Special Branch in the Malayan Emergency* has no light to shed on Batang Kali but does concede that at the time there was much mistrust between the Chinese community and the British.

"I had come over to Malaya as part of the re-occupying forces that took over as the Japanese surrendered. In 1946 I was appointed to the police force in Malaya." Comber served as OCPD (Officer in Charge of Police District) for Kuala Lumpur South (at that time Kuala Lumpur was divided into North and South zones for policing). As the threat of the CPM increased, he decided that learning a Chinese dialect might be crucial to the success of his mission.

The Emergency was a savage war in which an estimated 12,000 people died. Did Comber ever have to do anything he was ashamed of?

"Personally I didn't, nor did I order any men under my command to do so. But I certainly heard rumours about dubious interrogation techniques. Apparently the head of the Special Branch, Richard Craig, issued a pamphlet which referred to undesirable methods of obtaining information. I was taken aback when I heard that. But if my fellow colleagues knew anything, they kept it to themselves."

Indeed, secrecy was very much the order of the day as the colonial government maintained strict control over the

28

media to ensure that their viewpoint got through to the people.

As for the Batang Kali massacre, it was a matter that reared its ugly head from time to time. Soon after the incident, in 1949, an investigation by then Attorney General Sir Stafford Foster-Sutton concluded that the villagers would have escaped with their lives if not for the soldiers opening fire, yet no action was taken. In fact, only the soldiers themselves were questioned as witnesses, while no villagers were asked for their testimony. The hush-up echoed that of another British colonial massacre in Amritsar in 1919, when Colonel Reginald Dyer ordered the shooting deaths of hundreds of unarmed Indian civilians.

Following a similar incident in the late 1960s in Vietnam in which US troops, unable to distinguish friend from foe, slaughtered villagers in My Lai, the Batang Kali incident was revisited by British newspaper *The People.* Then British Secretary of State for Defence Denis Healey set up a team to investigate the incident. But it was soon dropped for lack of evidence, despite statements from former members of the patrol making it clear that they had been ordered to lie about the killings at the original 1949 investigation!

Still later, in 1992, a BBC documentary about the killings, *In Cold Blood*, was aired making it obvious that a travesty had occurred, not just with the killings but with the cover-up. Journalists Ian Ward and Norma Miraflor also painstakingly put together *Slaughter And Deception At Batang Kali*, another piece of investigation that endorses this viewpoint. MCA Public Services and Complaints Department Head Michael Chong got involved with the case during the filming of *In Cold Blood.*

"It is not only me who was fighting this case," he said. "Over the years many fought it. Even Tunku Abdul Rahman fought it before Independence. But when I came to it in 1992 it was forgotten. All the time there had been a ding-dong and finally after a change of government in the UK the case was closed. In late 1992, a group of BBC journalists came down with a few ex-Scots Guards who were all in their seventies or eighties. They were not involved in the massacre but had been asked by the Commanding Officer to help with the post-massacre clean-up. They came and asked the villages to remove the bodies. After so many years they feel bad."

Chong was outraged by the injustice and decided to act. "We were asked by foreign journalists why we didn't take up the case. Along with the lawyers Vincent Lim and Lim Choon Kin, I took an interest. We went to see the place and met the survivors. In 1993 we called a press conference and we lodged a police report in Batang Kali with the victims. After that we drafted a letter to Her Majesty the Queen to investigate this old case and seek for justice. We went to see the High Commissioner HC White and were given his assurance that it would be passed to her.

"Meanwhile, we also worked with police. I was cautioned by the Malaysian police not to stir up this sentiment. To be very frank, our MCA leaders also asked me why I wanted to bring up this old matter. They neither supported me or were against me at first. Later on they gave me their moral support.

"For me this was never about publicity. I just wanted justice for the victims. I want the British government to recognise and admit that such incidents happened. They were all shot in the back of the head from a close distance. This is cold-blooded murder. They were never communists, but simple rubber tappers. They were not even sympathisers."

News editor Eddie Chua has covered crime for four major newspapers and was often close to the action. He was one of the reporters who worked closely with Chong on the case. "I was one of those who broke the story in the 1990s," he recalled. "Suddenly it became hot news and we really thought we would see developments. I was so keen on it I wanted to go to the UK and follow up with the Scots Guards, many of whom were still alive then. But I didn't get the right backing. In fact when we pushed and pushed, we met resistance and finally the story got dropped."

In 2012, Martin Vengadesan visited Batang Kali along with reporter Lim Chia Ying and spoke to a number of people affected by the massacre. It was a moving, unforgettable experience.

Lim Kok was about nine years old when he received news from the villagers that his father Lim Tian Swee had been decapitated and his dismembered head thrown into the river. "My father was headman of a rubber tapping estate — which was managed by a distant granduncle — who paid

Batang Kali, the river where the severed heads were thrown.
The Star file image (courtesy of Star Media Group).

salaries to the workers and looked after their welfare," said Lim, who by then was 73.

"He was my family's sole breadwinner. Life became tough for us all after father was gone. My mother had to seek the help of friends and relatives to raise us. I was sad yet I was also too young to understand any fear that came from the implications of my father's killing. Thanks to some funds and assistance from my granduncle, we managed to provide my father with a proper burial according to Buddhist rites even if the head could not be traced."

Lim Kok faithfully returns to the burial ground every year to pay respects to his father during Qing Ming (Tomb Sweeping Day). "My only wish is to be granted sufficient compensation and a proper apology for the misdeed that was unleashed against the 24 people. Coming back to Batang Kali is a grim reminder of the suffering and misery that we had to endure and the poverty that my siblings especially had to grow up with. After all these decades, we are hopeful that fairness and justice will prevail," he said.

Chong Koon Ying was 11 when her father, Chong Man, was shot while being held captive. "We heard a lot of gunshots being fired but we were not allowed to bear witness to what happened. I could see thick smoke billowing right after. Later, a lorry just whisked all the families away and we were not allowed to even go back to our houses to collect our clothes or belongings.

"We were left homeless overnight after our village was razed. Some people who saw us seated aimlessly on the streets took pity and sought out a decrepit house for our shelter. Because there were so many families cramped in one small unit, the children had to sleep on the floor while my mother slept seated on a stool."

Choking with emotion, Chong, 73, said she was married off at 16 while her siblings had to be given away for adoption as her family had nothing else to survive on. "We had to be split up when food and everything else became scarce," said Chong. "I tried finding my sister but to no avail. And when I found my brother, he was badly beaten up. I can never forget how my heartbroken mum died when she found out."

Chong said her children and grandchildren have been told of the savage murders which tore families apart and left traumatised women and children incapacitated. "What else can I ask for except for cash compensation? My parents are gone; at the very least, monies should be paid for the hardship and our pain, although no amount (of cash) can bring them back."

There is an interesting story surrounding the last surviving witness Tham Yong, who passed away in 2010. Tham's fiance was one of the dead victims whose brother was the one who fainted and survived the massacre. It turns out that Tham Yong married him instead.

Another witness is Wong Then Loy, who was just eight when he helped his dad collect the corpses a week after they were killed. "The bodies had rotted and others had dried up; some even had huge maggots crawling out," recalled Wong, 73, when interviewed.

"As a kid, I wasn't afraid of seeing the worms since I was used to following my father deep into the jungles. Of course, I also didn't know exactly what took place except there were dead bodies. My father related to me the stories later while I also gathered bits of excerpts from wives of the deceased and some neighbours."

His father helped to engrave names on the tombstones after the dead had been identified by their relatives. There were some who remained unidentified and they were buried together in one plot — a group of young men who had barely touched 20. "I sometimes wonder how the families were able to identify and recognise the bodies as many were dried stiff by the time we were allowed to collect them," he said.

Eventually, the British government relented and agreed to hear the case. In May 2012, four claimants left for London for a judicial review application. They were Chong

Nyok Keyu (son of Tham Yong), Loh Ah Choi (nephew to the first massacred victim Luo Wei-Nan), Lim Kok and Wooi Kum Thai.

Lawyer Quek Ngee Meng was part of a new generation of Malaysians who felt that there should be no statute of limitations on justice. "Back in 2004 my father, the late Quek Jin Teck, used to visit the hot springs in Ulu Yam near Batang Kali to treat an illness. He used to go from Serdang to that area and eventually bought a house in Ulu Yam. He listened to the stories of villagers.

"It is still a public topic there more than 60 years on. Those killed were from Ulu Yam. If you go there you won't miss the cemetery. Every Qing Ming, they go back. They still feel it. It is still a stigma. The official account says they are suspected of being bandits. When we followed the case, we found a lot of cover-ups. We have evidence that the British High Commission in Malaysia used its political influence to get the case dropped!"

But what can be accomplished after so many years?

"I think the first thing is an admission and an apology," said Quek. "The victim's families also lost a lot of breadwinners so we are also seeking compensation. When pursuing this case, the famous human rights law firm Bindmans backed us and was willing to procure legal aid. Over here there are still about five witnesses to what happened. In Britain some soldiers are still alive, but every few years there will be less.

"There are many who have passed away, most recently Tham Yong in 2010. But we documented their testimony.

Before Bindmans granted us legal aid they checked if we are poor enough. Also whether there is any merit in the case."

Quek said cases like Batang Kali were not necessarily unique at the time. "There were many other cases of injustice during the Emergency. You must understand this was at a time when the British thought all Chinese were communists. The Chinese had to prove they were not communists. Even in such circumstances you must follow the rule of law. If they are identified by informers they should have been detained and questioned. But they were not."

Quek made a final point about the trial process. "We made a lot of progress with the Labour government, but after the Conservative-led coalition under David Cameron took power, they were not so straightforward with us. They have made a lot of representation using technical points trying to claim that it was the Selangor government who had jurisdiction and we should take action against the Sultan instead of them! This is a landmark case with an individual suing the British government."

Unfortunately, by September 2012, the attempt to revive the case seemed written off for good. The High Court ruled that a public inquiry into the killings will not be able to reach any credible conclusion, given the length of time that had passed. A British government spokesman commented: "We did not feel that the interests of justice would have been served by spending significant sums on further investigations for which there have been a number of previous enquiries."

This was upheld by the UK's Supreme Court in November 2015, which issued the judgement that the government was not obliged to hold a public inquiry because even though it may have been a war crime, it had occurred too long ago.

VERDICT Through a combination of time and bureaucratic obstruction, this case was swept under the carpet for more than 70 years. British forces killed unarmed and innocent Malayan villagers and escaped censure.

5

GURNEY'S FINAL DRIVE

Date : October 6, 1951
Crime : The British High Commissioner is shot to death
in an ambush

Details: The early 1950s was still a period of frenzied activity in Malaya as physical battles for territory and political battles for control of the nation's destiny raged. The Malayan Emergency had witnessed many heated flashpoints like the Bukit Kepong stand-off on February 23, 1950, between police officers and communist fighters, which saw more than 20 fatalities on each side. On December 3, 1949, the British governor of Sarawak Sir Duncan Stewart was stabbed to death by teenage nationalist Rosli Dhobi.

But the killing of Britain's top man in Malaysia was the most sensational and high-profile incident of all. Sir Henry Gurney had come to Malaya fresh from another challenging assignment overseeing the chaotic independence of modern Palestine and Israel and was tasked with managing the undeclared war against the communists. By the time he arrived in Malaya, the Communist Party of Malaya (CPM) was on the back foot, driven underground and sorely affected by many losses and defections. However, they were still capable of causing great damage. Three years into his tour, Gurney and his wife Lady Isabel were being driven up to Fraser's Hill escorted by an armoured scout car and a Land Rover. Another van in the convoy was unfortunately unable to accompany them. As they neared the base station known as Fraser's Hill Gap, they were ambushed by a group of 20–30 communist cadres led by Siew Mah.

Gurney's driver was shot instantly in the head and his private secretary DJ Staples had to reach over to grab the wheel to prevent the car from falling off the edge into a ravine. Heavy fire soon made it clear that Gurney's party was vastly outnumbered and outgunned. In a move of great chivalry, Gurney opened the door and stepped out into the firing line where he was instantly cut down in a slew of bullets. The firing went on for 10 minutes until the guerrillas withdrew. Lady Gurney and Staples found Gurney's body in a ditch by the side of the road.

It seemed like a great victory for the communists and was thought at the time to be a possible turning point in the Emergency. As it turned out, Gurney's death was to have a very negative effect on their struggle. Leon Comber said: "At the time of the killing, I was the honorary ADC (aide-de-camp) to Sir Henry Gurney. However, I was in Johor when he was murdered. Gurney was a liberal and a nice man, whereas his successor (Field Marshal) Sir Gerald

Templer, was much more dictatorial and determined to finish the communist threat once and for all.

"I do feel that Templer is given too much credit for winning the war against the communists, because the brilliant plan that defeated them was devised by General Sir Harold Briggs. It was he who combined military, police and civil administration in a way that could effectively counter the CPM."

The Briggs Plan was put into operation soon after Gurney's death. The main strategic aim was to cut off communist forces from their rural support network, by forcibly relocating half a million people — most of them ethnic Chinese — into fortified New Villages. The other aim of the plan was to win over their hearts and minds, by providing settlers with healthcare and education, as well as homes with running water and electricity.

The nature of Gurney's death also helped galvanise public opinion. The legend of him stepping out to meet his fate and draw fire away from his wife was one that spread. Professor Khoo said: "There were plenty of rumours during this time too. Some alleged that members of Gurney's kitchen staff had given away his plans to the communists and that is why they were able to wait there for him with such a powerful force."

As for the communists themselves, CPM Secretary General Chin Peng denied that it was a well-planned ambush. In his memoir, *My Side of History*, he said that the group leader Siew Mah had no idea who was about to fall in his lap and that the party only found out whom they had killed through news reports. Khoo, however, feels that Chin Peng's denials are to be taken with a pinch of salt. Incidentally, Siew Mah was murdered by his own men eight years after Gurney's killing.

VERDICT No one was ever caught and tried for Gurney's murder. His name and his sacrifice live on in Malaysian institutions to this day.

6

THE GLAMOROUS GUERRILLA

Date : July, 1952
Crime : A beautiful woman is photographed in possession
of illegal firearms

Details: By 1952, it was becoming increasingly clear
that the communist threat was going to be defeated
militarily. But the detention of a young girl, Lee Meng,
and her subsequent trial brought the country back into
international spotlight.

Aged 26, Lee Meng (born Lee Ten Tai) had joined
the Communist Party of Malaya (CPM) during World War
II while still a teenager. She was active in underground
activities in the Ipoh area and claimed that her mother had
been detained by the Japanese during the war. When the
British came back and reasserted their colonial rule, Lee
Meng was one of those who continued the fight, indeed
assuming a leadership role despite her tender years.

Eventually she was captured by the British and tried for
possession of a hand grenade, which was a questionable

Lawyer DR Seevnivasagam made his name defending Lee Meng.

charge because she was not in possession of one at the time of her arrest. The trial proved a sensational one. Lee Meng's good looks and tale of woe made her a sympathetic figure and her lawyer, DR Seenivasagam, was about to prove himself one of the most engaging orators of the time.

No less than six former guerrillas testified against Lee Meng, saying that she was the woman photographed in a camp holding a grenade. When one of them said that he was a non-shooting participant in a raid which resulted in the death of two police officers in March 1949, Seenivasagam put him in his place by asking him if he was there for 'sightseeing'.

The defence hinged on a case of mistaken identity. Lee Meng simply denied being the guerrilla leader, saying that she was a simple schoolteacher and that it was another woman pictured in the photograph.

At that time, courts in Malaya operated under the Criminal Procedure Code of 1927 and 'assessors' judged cases that involved the death penalty. Lee Meng's case highlighted the weaknesses of the assessor system. Despite the ample testimony against her, she was initially found innocent by both 'local' assessors, which so outraged judge Justice J Thomson that he ordered a re-trial.

The second trial in September was presided over by Justice Pretheroe. This time around, a European assessor voted guilty and a local voted not guilty. Pretheroe leapt in to side with the European, and amidst uproar, Lee Meng was declared guilty and sentenced to death.

Professor Khoo said: "I need to point out that Chinese women were also involved in the political struggle. Compared to their Malay and Indian counterparts, Chinese women enjoyed greater freedoms. This case was widely followed and not just in Malaya. The English press covered it well. DR Seenivasagam made his name through this case and went on to become a political force in Perak with the People's Progressive Party, and he was much loved by the Chinese community. The people were not so much pro-Lee Meng or anti-Lee Meng, as they were curious about her."

Indeed, despite Lee Meng's protestations of innocence, her former head, CPM Secretary General Chin Peng confirmed in his autobiography that Lee Meng was indeed the woman in question and she did play a prominent role in coordinating guerrilla activities. Chin Peng was not particularly sympathetic to Lee Meng's plight blaming it on her reckless, careless nature, traits that were clearly not compatible with carrying out clandestine activities.

Despite the death sentence, the Lee Meng story was far from over. In February 1953, her lawyer Lim Phaik Gan, future Labour Party of Malaya candidate and ambassador, brought her case before a judicial committee of the Privy Council but to no avail. This was followed by the Communist Hungarian government of Matyas Rakosi offering to swap Edgar Sanders, a businessman serving 13 years for espionage, for her release. To top it all, more than 50 members of the UK parliament signed a petition to the Sultan of Perak, Sultan Sir Yusuf Izzuddin Shah, asking him to grant an unconditional pardon to Lee Meng.

These efforts were opposed by then UK Prime Minister Sir Winston Churchill, but Lee Meng's sentence was eventually commuted. After serving 11 years in Taiping Prison, she was repatriated to China in 1964 where she linked up with her former communist colleagues and married a powerful figure in Chen Tien. In 2007, the elderly Lee Meng made an emotional visit back to Malaysia.

VERDICT A product of her time, Lee Meng clearly was the organiser of terrorist activities in the Ipoh area and was lucky to go on to lead a normal life after serving 11 years in prison.

7

THE DISTRAUGHT WIDOW

Date : May 14, 1953
Crime : A young mother kills her two sons and attempts suicide

Details: A bloody war will invariably see the slaying of many innocents, no doubt viewed as 'collateral damage' by those who initiate hostilities. One of the more tragic documented cases of the Emergency is what happened to the Parsons family in Penang.

In May 1953, a member of the British Royal Air Force's Squadron 33 Flight Lieutenant DR Parsons was killed while carrying out a bomb strike on the Communist Party of Malaya (CPM). Parsons' wife, Elizabeth, 28, was understandably distraught when informed of his demise by Squadron Leader SCF Cooper. She began drinking heavily and openly questioned what her dead husband would do in the afterlife without her.

Cooper and his wife Winifred were keen to keep an eye on Elizabeth, who now found herself a widow with two young sons, Edmund, four, and Darryl, two. However, she assured them that she had regained her composure and they proceeded to dinner with some friends.

Later that night, they decided to check in on the Parsons family. As Cooper was to testify in court later, a chilling sight met their eyes. "I entered the passage and I saw a light in the bathroom. Mrs Parsons was standing by the bath. I entered the bathroom and saw both her wrists had been slashed. She was hysterical so I smacked her face and asked her to calm down. She said she had strangled both her children."

Winifred Cooper, unable to contain herself, burst out: "You fool! What have you done?"

These grisly findings were confirmed by Inspector Govindasamy who discovered the two lifeless bodies under mosquito nets covered with a sarong. The bodies showed signs of abrasions.

Elizabeth Parsons' wounds were tended to at the local hospital. She tried to stab herself there, but was once again prevented from carrying out her suicidal plan. Instead, she found herself in the Penang Sessions Court on trial for the murder of her children. She was the first white woman to go on trial for her life in Malaya since Ethel Proudlock some 40 years earlier.

The trial was necessarily an emotional one in which prosecutor DMK Grant and defence counsel IU Meek themselves had to master their emotions. Meek tried to persuade the assessors that Parsons had been of unsound mind. This was supported by the testimony of an RAF doctor who had administered her with sodium amytal. He said that it could have an unusual effect when combined with alcohol.

Grant, on the other hand, focused on the fact that Parsons had taken the time to write three letters, addressed to Cooper and other officers. He argued that this showed that however tragic the outcome, Elizabeth Parsons was in possession of her faculties at the time of the killings.

Ultimately, emotion won as a not guilty verdict was delivered to a tearful court.

VERDICT Elizabeth Parsons was found not guilty because of unsound mind at the time of the crimes. She vanished from these shores and started a new life under an assumed name.

8

THE MISSING MILLIONAIRE

Date : March 26, 1967
Crime : An American silk merchant vanishes while on holiday
in Cameron Highlands

Details: It is impossible to visit the idyllic hillside resort of
Cameron Highlands without coming face to face with the
legend of Jim Thompson. An American entrepreneur who
made his fortune in silk, Thompson went on holiday to
Cameron Highlands, took a stroll out in the jungle and
never returned.

Jim Thompson was a rich man and the fact that he had
once served in the US military as an intelligence officer
led to all manner of conspiracy theories regarding his
disappearance. Despite more than a hundred police
personnel and volunteers dispatched to look for him,
Thompson's whereabouts were never discovered.

Veteran journalist and former *The Star* Associate Editor
PK Katharason recalled: "We used to read about it. It was
much talked about at the time. The gossip was that he was

The late Jim Thompson. *The Star* file image (courtesy of Star Media Group).

still alive and living amongst the Orang Asli. Others said there might be a CIA link, or that he was taken to Thailand."

Professor Khoo offered a simpler explanation: "There was so much speculation, but I'm inclined to believe that he just wasn't well prepared and got lost in the jungle. We think of Cameron Highlands as quite a 'tame' place but there was certainly more than enough room back then for a man to meet his end and the body to lie undiscovered at the bottom of a ravine."

Thompson, who had just celebrated his 61st birthday, was staying at Moonlight Bungalow with friends. His decision to go for an afternoon walk after attending that morning's Easter service was not at all unusual. In fact, he and his friend Dr Ling Tien Gi had gone for a walk the day before and got lost for a while! When he did not return by nightfall, Dr Ling reported the matter to the police.

For the next few days, the search for Thompson escalated until it became one of the largest in Malaysian history. Most were confident that Thompson would be found alive as he had undergone jungle survival training before. But despite generous rewards for his return offered by his company The Thai Silk Company, friends and the police, Thompson was never found.

After more than 10 days of intensive search, the police finally took the decision to reduce their efforts. There were also many failed private expeditions, such as one led by Richard Noone — a former British intelligence officer who had also served as head of the Malayan Department of Aborigines (a forerunner to today's Department of Orang Asli Development (Jakoa)) — a few weeks after Thompson's disappearance.

Rumours persisted that Thompson had either been abducted or staged his own disappearance. Some were fearful that he had fallen into the hands of communist guerrillas, particularly given his alleged links to the CIA. Another twist in the tale occurred five months after his disappearance when his older sister, Katherine, was found bludgeoned to death in her home in Pennsylvania. Six years later, Noone died in Bangkok at the age of 55.

It's worth noting that Thompson's disappearance came less than a year after the sensational disappearance of Malaysia's High Commissioner to Australia Lim Yew Hock. Lim, who had served as Chief Minister of Singapore from 1956 to 1959, was appointed Malaysian High Commissioner in 1964 (during the brief period when Singapore was part of Malaysia).

However, in June 1966, he went missing and his wife and daughter appeared on television pleading for his safe return. Ten days later he was found alive and well, although apparently suffering from a form of amnesia, and unable to account for his whereabouts. There were also whispers that he had actually taken off to visit a stripper in Sydney!

As with many legendary cases, the mystery of Jim Thompson's disappearance looks destined to be unsolved. There have been investigative books and claims that some human bones discovered at a hospital near Cameron Highlands might be his. Others even maintained that he was spirited away to Tahiti!

VERDICT The simplest solution is the correct one ... that Thompson took a stroll and met an untimely end in such a manner that his body could not be found.

9

TOP COP KILLED

Date : June 7, 1974
Crime : The nation's most senior police officer is shot dead
in the heart of Kuala Lumpur

Details: One of Malaysia's most shocking killings involved the Inspector-General of Police (IGP) Abdul Rahman Hashim. The nation's top cop was slain while travelling to work in Lorong Raja Chulan, a victim of a planned assassination.

The shocking crime against Abdul Rahman was attributed to communist terrorists, but once again, not everything is so straightforward. Abdul Rahman was well known as a man of principle and authority, who was not prepared to accord high-ranking politicians carte blanche just because of their position. He was also committed to improving the welfare of police officers who had borne the brunt of the communist insurgency.

What is certain is that Abdul Rahman's killing occurred at a time of renewed communist aggression. Even though

The late IGP Abdul Rahman Hashim. *The Star* file image (courtesy of Star Media Group).

it was clear that the Communist Party of Malaya (CPM) was not gaining ground in Malaysia, communist parties in Indochina were enjoying great success. The movement in Malaysia, which itself had splintered after some bloody internal purges, was ordered to step up its activity and had done so largely through a string of attacks against police personnel.

The killing of Abdul Rahman was no doubt the most high profile of all. On that fateful morning, Abdul Rahman had set off from his home in Jalan Kia Peng and was due to attend the Thai-Malaysian General Border Committee meeting at Federal Hotel on Jalan Bukit Bintang. However, he made an unscheduled detour to the police headquarters in Bukit Aman. When his official Mercedes cut through Lorong Raja Chulan, he was gunned down in a hail of bullets, allegedly fired by two assassins who then made their escape. His driver, Sergeant Omar, escaped with light injuries, making it likely that it was a targeted killing.

Abdul Rahman's son Najib Rahman was then a junior reporter who happened upon the site soon after the shooting. Anyone who has read his harrowing description of his arrival upon the scene and discovery of his father's death at the Kuala Lumpur General Hospital can hardly fail to be moved by his grief.

There was a string of circumstances that make the killing and the subsequent search for justice somewhat suspect. Despite a statement by former IGP Musa Hassan to the effect that communist terrorists Lim Woon Chong and Ng Foo Nam were charged for the crime, it remains a fact that the Prosecution eventually withdrew those charges before both men were executed for a different crime.

The late Democratic Action Party (DAP) national chairman and famed lawyer Karpal Singh was the defence counsel for Lim. Speaking in 2012, he vividly recounted his experiences in the case: "These two fellows were part of the assault team of the Malayan National Liberation Front, a communist front. In fact my fellow, Lim, was the head.

"This was a time when lots of detectives were being shot dead, found in drains and that sort of thing. They were charged under the Essential Security Cases (Amendment) Regulations of 1975, which I argued was invalid. It was quite an eventful trial. I remember at the end of the trial, my chap threw his slipper at the judge!

"During my meetings with Lim he told me, 'You are a

The author Martin Vengadesan with the late Karpal Singh,
who shared his experiences.

good man, you are trying to help people. But DAP's way is
very difficult. The only way is the gun.' I said, 'Forget that.
We differ in our ideology also!'"

Aside from the trial of Abdul Rahman, Lim and Ng were
also tried for the murder of Perak Chief Police Officer
(CPO) Khoo Chong Kong and his driver Sergeant Yeong
Peng Chong who were killed in Ipoh on November 13,
1975, a year and a half after Abdul Rahman's killing. It was
for that murder that they were found guilty on March 22,
1978, and eventually hanged.

"Just before he was hanged I went to see him," recalled
Karpal.

"He was very cool. He said, 'Thank you for having
defended me. All of us are going to die, it's just a matter
of when. And my time is tomorrow.' He said to me, 'Now

look here, the CPO in Perak and the other officer. I did it. I deserve to die for that. But the IGP I don't know anything about his murder. I wasn't even in the state. You must clear my name of that charge.'

"I made a last-minute application and the judge Harun Hashim, who was quite a judge, was apparently willing to look at it, but then the Prosecution withdrew the charge regarding Abdul Rahman's murder.

"This to me is still quite shocking. Think about it. The IGP was killed. If you can't solve the murder of your own top policeman, it doesn't say much for your abilities!" claimed Karpal.

Professor Khoo concurred: "In the end the story about the communists was what people were persuaded to believe. At the time, there was a tendency to blame the communists for everything. They were the only ones who knew how to use firearms and were organised. But this is not like Henry Gurney's killing. Gurney was believed to have been betrayed by his own cook, and he got out of the car to draw fire away from his wife and was killed by the communists. In this case there are some critical unanswered questions."

If Abdul Rahman was not slain by the communists, then who killed him? Some say that he had ruffled the feathers of powerful politicians, others allege that the secret societies had decided to go after him. There is no doubt that Abdul Rahman knew that there were people out to get him. It is said that on the day of his death, he was due to sign a life insurance policy worth RM1 million.

It must be emphasised, however, that the official explanation is still that he was assassinated by the communists.

VERDICT Some 40 years after his death, questions remain over the official narrative of the killing of Abdul Rahman Hashim.

10

THE ROBIN HOOD
OF SENTUL

Date : February 16, 1976
Crime: A notorious criminal is finally captured after
a shootout with the police

Details: Botak Chin (born Wong Swee Chin) is arguably
Malaysia's most famous criminal. He made his name
through a string of 'supernatural' feats which accompanied
his violent exploits. Despite being on the run, he was
widely supported by the local population and even when
he was finally apprehended, the circumstances added to
his folklore. After a failed attempt to bust out of death row,
Botak Chin was finally hanged.

The son of a Malayan Railways employee, Botak Chin
grew up in the Jalan Ipoh/Sentul area. However, after the
death of his mother his life fell apart. A Form 3 dropout,
he flirted with normal life, working as a fishmonger before
drifting into a life of crime, something which he attributed

to having to defend himself against the real gangsters. In the late 1960s, while still a teenager, he had a spell in the Sak Pak Lok (360) gang before eventually heading his own gang. In 1969, he was imprisoned in connection with a spate of armed robberies.

In 1974, he was freed from prison and set about forming a new gang. Its philosophy wasn't a typical one, as Chin tried to ensure that his members were all committed to sharing their spoils with the extended community. In fact, his nickname Botak comes not from any lack of hair (he indeed was not bald) but from his commitment to helping the downtrodden ... *Bantu Orang Tak Ada Kerja*!

Professor Khoo was not convinced. "Botak Chin was a thoroughly corrupt and crooked individual but he understood how to win people's hearts with a few gestures. There were quite a few people who admired Botak Chin and ascribed all sorts of powers and motives to him. The press indirectly also helped build up the myth about the man.

"Botak Chin and a few trusted lieutenants built up a reputation by hitting other gangs. His famous hits involved an illegal gambling den, a mahjong gang working out of a temple, a bank in Jalan Imbi and the daily profits of the Turf Club. Despite his many violent acts, Botak Chin became known for his intelligence and generosity to the poor."

PK Katharason recalled: "To the poor people of the time, Botak Chin was more of a Robin Hood. His image was that of someone who robbed the rich and helped the poor.

Botak Chin after his arrest. *The Star* file image (courtesy of Star Media Group).

There were a lot of gangsters around during the era who tried to portray that image, not just him. Before him there was the Sea King of Pangkor and another chap called Malai Chai, who somehow knew how to gain support amongst the people while committing their crimes.

"All the racial communities liked Botak Chin. Even the lower-ranked Malay cops would not tell you where he is. And even though he was not so good-looking he had girlfriends everywhere. He had a lot of talismans and it was said that he took frequent trips to Thailand to boost his immunity through black magic.

"There was indeed a famous escape from death in Segambut, when he was involved in a shootout with the police. His car was full of bullets but he emerged unscathed. It was impossible, however, for Botak Chin to go on unpunished. The death of his chief lieutenants, Ng Cheng Wong (Ah Wong), Chau Kuan (Ah Kuan) and Seh Chai, within a short period of time weakened his organisation, but rather than back down, Botak Chin grew more daring, engaging in many confrontations with the cops."

Professor Shamsul said: "Botak Chin was not alone, but the ringleader working in a trusted group. He avoided death so many times that people started to say he had supernatural powers. I believe that he simply had a good underground network of informers, maybe even within the police. He had good brains and knew how to project a certain image. The media also built him up, and after a while maybe the urban legends about him started to help his cause."

Botak Chin's exploits also helped build up a confrontation with crime-busting police officer DSP S Kulasingam. By early 1976, however, his number was up. In what appeared to be a frame-up, Botak Chin was lured to a sawmill in Jalan Ipoh and found himself surrounded by police on the night of February 16. Despite being shot six times, his life was not under serious threat. It was enough, however, for him to be arrested.

Dr M Mahadevan is a former government chief psychiatrist and founder of the Malaysian Psychiatric Association. A pioneer in his field, he studied Botak Chin at length before deciding he was fit to be tried. "He was not just any common man, but a misguided distorted genius who was a victim of his own circumstances," said Mahadevan. "I studied him on our own CCTV for 18 days at our facility."

"He was very charismatic and told me that he had a tough life and was bullied and had to fight back. Soon the other inmates were offering to do work for him. He had no end of female admirers who were calling every other day. Eventually someone sent a bullet to him, and I had to remove him before they broke him out of Tanjung Rambutan. I still remember him saying, 'I did not kill anyone, I executed those who were bad.'

"But in my final analysis I had to say that he was 'not mad, but bad'."

Eventually, Botak Chin went to trial facing three charges under the Internal Security Act in May 1980. He was sentenced to death by the High Court in 1980.

His last hurrah was to make a daring prison break on January 1, 1981. While in isolation on death row, he managed to get hold of a weapon and stabbed two prison wardens. He was eventually apprehended and within six months, on June 11, the invincible Botak Chin was executed by hanging.

VERDICT Botak Chin was a charismatic individual, but also a violent criminal — despite the heroic motives accorded to his actions.

11

THE DOUBLE SIX CRASH

Date : June 6, 1976
Crime : The Chief Minister of Sabah is among 12 killed
in a plane crash

Details: One June 6, 1976, a Nomad plane operated by Sabah Air left Labuan for Kota Kinabalu, carrying on board many of the state's most important figures. On its approach to Kota Kinabalu the plane crashed in the district of Sembulan, claiming the lives of 12 people.

The Double Six Crash, as it came to be known, had a monumental impact on Sabahans at the time. Fuad Stephens, who had just returned to the post of Chief Minister of Sabah, was the most high-profile victim on board, but there were many others including state ministers Salleh Sulong, Peter Mojuntin and Chong Thien Vun, as well as Fuad's eldest son Johari Stephens.

Given the political implications of the crash and its timing, which was just 53 days after Fuad replaced long-time Chief Minister Mustapha Harun, the crash became a focal point for many Sabahans who felt that their state was being undermined by federal authorities. Even Fuad's successor Harris Salleh found himself the victim of nasty rumours that he had foreknowledge of the incident. In fact, this rumour resurfaced when yet another former Sabah Chief Minister Yong Teck Lee brought it up, and was promptly sued by Harris.

On March 1, 2012, Yong was ordered to pay RM1million by the High Court in Kota Kinabalu after being charged with defaming Harris. Yong had called for another probe into the crash following reports quoting former Finance Minister Tengku Razaleigh Hamzah as saying that he was already buckled up on the ill-fated plane when Harris asked him to disembark and join another Nomad flight to Banggi Island to inspect a cattle farm.

The Daily Express on June 7, 1976, breaking news of the Chief Minister's death.

Harris' response was that Razaleigh had never been scheduled to fly to Kota Kinabalu with Stephens but had intended to fly with then Sarawak Chief Minister Rahman Yaakub to Kudat on the second Nomad plane and then by helicopter to Banggi.

Former Suhakam (National Human Rights Commission) vice-chairman Simon Sipaun was one of those who has called for a new investigation into the tragedy, also citing the remarks by Tengku Razaleigh. The coroner at the time of the initial investigation was Ansari Abdullah and he returned an open verdict. However, there was an implication that human error and the overloading of the plane were to blame.

Professor Shamsul was personally affected by the incident. "It was fate, just a terrible accident. There was a very thorough technical investigation, and I think the plane was just overloaded. My roommate Ishak Atan was on board. He was private secretary to Tengku Razaleigh, who was supposed to be aboard but at the last moment, they switched and it was Ishak who lost his life. It was just fated."

PK Katharason said: "Because Razaleigh was supposed to be on the plane, and Harris asked him to fly with him, Harris has had to contend with much speculation through the years. At the trial the Australian experts said the plane was overloaded so it is accepted as that."

The family of Fuad was understandably deeply affected by the tragedy. However, a different element is detailed in a book they commissioned, PJ Granville-Edge's *The Sabahan: The Life & Death of Tun Fuad Stephens.*

Fuad Stephens' daughter Faridah told us: "At the time they said that the plane was overloaded and the crash was therefore due to 'human error'. The team that came from Australia to investigate the crash also said that no Nomads had crashed before this one. We later discovered that this was not true. There had been a Nomad crash in 1973. In fact, in August 1976, just two months after the crash, another Nomad crashed during tests in Avalon, just outside Melbourne."

Faridah continued: "In 1995, a documentary by the Australian Broadcasting Corporation called *Four Corners* focused on the poor track record of the Nomad plane. The Australian military had refused to fly it by that time and dubbed it 'the widow maker' because it was very unstable. The documentary refers to a 10-volume report on the Nomad, but the report seems not to have been made public. One of the implications of the report is that there is a flaw with the Nomad's tailplane apparently which causes the plane to spiral downward when the plane is coming in to land. These planes fall out of clear skies."

Indeed, a study of the Nomad's aviation history tells its own tale. Out of the 172 Nomads that were built, no less than 32 suffered hull loss crashes! As recently as January 2010, a Nomad crash in the Philippines killed eight military personnel, while in 2009 there were other fatal crashes in Lop Buri, Thailand and Bulungan, Indonesia.

Many felt that the federal government had tried to replace state leaders in Sarawak (Stephen Kalong Ningkan) and Sabah (Fuad Stephens and later Joseph Pairin Kitingan) with more compliant individuals.

Faridah said: "They have done it repeatedly since Malaysia was formed. However, while Fuad Stephens was removed as CM in 1964, he was also backed by West Malaysia against Usno's Mustapha in the 1976 election. I guess I prefer to think that while our politicians can be manipulative, they weren't murderers."

So why didn't people of the time give credence to the report on the plane crash and why are the conspiracy theories still popular? Faridah said: "I think the timing of the crash just 53 days after Fuad won the elections made it appear like someone wanted them all dead. Bombs had also gone off in Kota Kinabalu after Berjaya won. There were a lot of accusations and rumours flying around for a long time and there still are more than 40 years on.

"We will never be absolutely certain what happened after all these years. The government aircraft factory people who were set the task of investigating it were not entirely truthful. And the evidence has of course disappeared. I would still say that the likeliest explanation is the crash occurred because of the faulty plane."

VERDICT Despite sinister rumours, the most compelling case put forward is that of the poor safety track record of the Nomad plane which, in addition, was overloaded, leading to the fatal crash.

12

THE TANJUNG KUPANG TRAGEDY

Date : December 4, 1977
Crime : Flight MH653 crashes after being deliberately diverted from its course

Details: In December 1977, flight MH653 took off from Penang on a routine flight to Subang, which was then the country's main airport. In mid-air it was diverted to Singapore. Before it reached its destination, however, it crashed into a swamp in Tanjung Kupang, Johor killing all 100 on board.

Among the 93 passengers were Agricultural Minister Ali Haji Ahmad, Public Works Department Chief Mahfuz Khalid, former Penang Deputy Chief Minister Ooh Chooi Cheng, rugby international Brian Pestana and Cuban Ambassador to Japan Mario Garcia Inchaustegui.

Investigations revealed that as the flight was nearing its destination, crew reported to air traffic personnel at

Subang that an unidentified hijacker had assumed control of the craft. It was then diverted beyond Subang to fly to Singapore. However, as it was making its way there a fatal confrontation occurred, leading to a fiery crash.

At first there was complete shock and disbelief but the recovery of the flight's black box gave some positive indications as to the cause of the tragedy. The pilot Captain GK Ganjoor, an Indian national, had in fact announced to passengers and crew that there was a hijacker on board. The hijacker then asked for all radio contact to be cut off. The conversation among the captain, flight officer and hijacker indicates that the hijacker was not properly prepared and had no clear plans about what to do.

The pilot and crew took pains to be courteous to him. "You relax, sir, we'll do exactly what you order us to, we are not going to do anything funny," they told him. But the hijacker was highly strung and paranoid about others entering the cockpit. He kept threatening the pilots and disbelieved whatever they told him. He was not sure where to land despite being informed there was limited fuel. "You bluff!" he cried. Eventually, there were sounds of a scuffle and the hijacker shot both the captain and flight officer despite their pleas.

"The government tried to blame it on the Japanese Red Army (JRA)," said a source close to the case. "Two years earlier in August 1975, there had been a hostage crisis in August 1975, when members of the JRA stormed the AIA building on Jalan Ampang, Kuala Lumpur, and took more than 50 hostages. The 1970s was also a time when

Minister Ali Haji Ahmad died at Tanjung Kupang. *The Star* image (courtesy of Star Media Group).

many planes were hijacked so when this happened people naturally thought it was another terrorist move.

"But actually when you hear the black box recordings it was revealed not to be so. The hijacker was not part of a group of Japanese terrorists. He was a desperate lone ranger acting irrationally. Not only that, he was part of the entourage of one of the senior government officials!"

PK Katharason led investigative reports that highlighted the lax security at Bayan Lepas airport, showcasing just how easy it was to smuggle weapons onto a plane. "The indication was that the crash was caused because the crew was fatally incapacitated, leaving the plane 'professionally uncontrolled.'

"Officially, no firm conclusion over the identity of the hijacker was ever established legally, but those who were near the case were very aware. It was covered up because the hijacker was part of the group of officials onboard."

VERDICT Officially the case remains unsolved, but sources make it clear that the hijacker was a Malaysian who was part of the group of officials on board.

13

THE SLAYING OF A BEAUTY QUEEN

Date : April 6, 1979
Crime : A former Miss Malaysia runner-up is found
           stabbed to death

Details: One of Malaysia's most sensational murder trials involved the death of beauty queen Jean Perera Sinnappa. A former Miss Malaysia runner-up, she was a widowed mother of three who was found stabbed to death in her car in an isolated turn-off point off the Federal Highway in Subang. Even more surprising was the fact that her brother-in-law, S Karthigesu, was found unconscious behind the car.

Psychology lecturer Karthigesu, who confessed to being in a romantic relationship with his late brother's widow, soon came under suspicion. In a sensational trial, he was charged with her murder, found guilty and sentenced to death. Perhaps even more sensationally, he was later freed after a key witness admitted to lying on the stand!

The facts of the case certainly seemed suspicious. Karthigesu said that he and Jean were returning to Klang

Front page of *The Star* on April 8, 1979, carrying news of Jean's shocking murder (courtesy of Star Media Group).

from a night out when he stopped off at a lonely junction to relieve himself. He then claims that he was knocked unconscious. Two engineers who were working for Malaysia Airlines which was then based at the nearby Subang airport came across their car. They saw the figure of Karthigesu lying near it and called the police.

When the police arrived, they found a much more gruesome sight inside the car. Jean Perera was found dead after having been stabbed 10 times. No valuables were taken, ruling out robbery as a motive. The police were surprised to discover that apart from being found unconscious, Karthigesu was relatively unharmed.

It was quite a sensation when he was charged with the crime a month later and by the time he stood trial on June 16, 1980, the whole nation was fixated on the case.

To this day, many who have met Karthigesu comment on how gentle his mannerisms were, and how patient and kind he seemed. From veteran journalists to teachers he trained and even hardened lawyers, many were moved to support his cause.

Still, the circumstances of the case were heavily against him. Firstly, why was he relatively unharmed while Jean was stabbed so viciously? In fact, the doctor who first examined him gave testimony saying that there was no sign of any trauma or injury on Karthigesu's head that would explain his being unconscious. In addition, based on the testimony of witnesses Ramly Othman and Abdul Wahad Abu Amin, who happened upon the scene at different times, it appeared as if Karthigesu had shifted his position while supposedly knocked out!

Secondly, at the time of the crime, it had only been four months since his brother, chemist S Sinappa, was killed in a car crash on New Year's Eve, and yet Karthigesu was already talking of marrying Jean. It was even hinted that Karthigesu had always been in love with his brother's wife.

Thirdly, during the course of the trial, allegations surfaced that Jean had been having an extramarital relationship with a Dr Narada Warnasurya, a Sri Lankan national. Some 19 letters, purportedly from the doctor to Jean, were introduced as evidence in court and compounded the scandal with lurid sexual details.

Finally, and perhaps most damningly, Jean's relative Bandhulananda Jayatilake testified that 10 days after the murder, he was at Karthigesu's house when the police came to question the latter. He said that when the police left, Karthigesu had lost his cool and ranted about Jean, saying "the bitch did not deserve to live."

Psychology lecturer, S Karthigesu. *The Star* file image (courtesy of Star Media Group).

The Prosecution convincingly argued that the mild-mannered Karthigesu had snapped and killed Jean while overcome by jealous rage. The Defence, on the other hand, tried to portray Karthigesu as a gentle man devoted to his family. They claimed that he had been attacked by unknown assailants who had gone on to kill Jean. They questioned why there was no blood splatter at all on Karthigesu if he was indeed the killer, and also why no murder weapon was found at the scene.

At that time, Malaysia had a jury system and by a vote of 5-2 Karthigesu was found guilty of the murder and sentenced to death.

PK Katharason recalled: "An interesting story which not many people are aware of is that Karthigesu and Botak Chin met in prison. They were on death row at the same time and there was a lot of public interest in both of their cases. Both men were supposed to be charmers, but we can only speculate as to what happened at their meeting and whether or not they charmed each other!"

In most cases, an appeal is nothing more than a

formality. However, when Karthigesu made his appeal, Jayatilake suddenly retracted his story, saying that he had not told the truth on the stand. Due to this confession, Karthigesu was sensationally acquitted while Jayatilake was sentenced to 10 years' jail after pleading guilty to a perjury charge. Although still a young man in his thirties, he was to die two years later while still serving his sentence. It was even speculated that he knew he was dying at the time he changed his story.

To this day, the Jean Perera case rouses strong emotions. Lawyer Y Sivaloganathan said: "It had all the ingredients of a Shakespearean drama and was quite possibly the most sensational murder trial in the country. Jean Perera was well known at the time. She was vivacious with striking eyes."

As with many cases nowadays, Karthigesu's involvement in the crime or lack thereof could quite easily have been proven with the forensic tools we have available these days, but back then, DNA testing simply did not exist. At that time, one of Malaysia's most famous police dogs was put on the case!

Despite Karthigesu's eventual release, the murder case continues to fascinate. A book, *The Murder of a Beauty Queen*, was written by Alex Josey while a documentary, *Jean Perera: The Beauty Queen Murder*, was produced in 2009. Opinions remain divided as to who her murderer actually was, or if the right man was convicted and then wrongly freed.

VERDICT Jean Perera Sinnappa's murder remains officially unsolved.

14

LONG LIVE KING GHAZ

Date : January 11, 1982
Crime : A plane crashes in the jungle and Foreign Minister
Ghazali Shafie is the only survivor

Details: In the early 1980s, a small plane piloted by then Malaysian Foreign Minister Ghazali Shafie crashed into a mountainous jungle in Pahang. A shocked nation listened raptly as the media announced the death of the man known as King Ghaz, his pilot and his bodyguard.

But then came an even bigger shock … the possibility that Ghazali had not perished in the crash after all!

PK Katharason was right in the thick of it. "*The Star* wrote the first edition saying that King Ghaz was dead. It was only later that we changed it to 'feared dead'. In fact, Martin Vengadesan went with *The Star* photographer Andrew Chong on a late night drive to Kuala Lipis to show his first cousin that the final edition did not say he had died. Still, King Ghaz was a master dramatist who wanted to fight Dr Mahathir Mohamad at the time for the prime

Front page of *The Star* on January 11, 1982, amended to say 'Minister feared dead' (courtesy of Star Media Group).

minister's job. The world was told that he was dead and we really believed it at the time."

News then began to emerge that Ghazali's body was not found among the wreckage of the six-seater Cessna plane that went down at Kampung Janda Baik, near Genting Highlands, in the jungles of Pahang. The bodies of his pilot Vergis Chacko and security aide Charon Daam were discovered at the site, still strapped to their seats in the upside-down plane wreckage. Ghazali and his team had been flying from Kuala Lumpur to Kuala Lipis in Pahang, where he was the local MP.

A massive manhunt was launched and after 28 hours in the jungle, Ghazali emerged barely harmed. Upon being rescued, he famously said, "I'm alive and walking. God is great." He said that he had ejected from the aircraft just before it crashed.

Ghazali's safe recovery was not, however, without its own problems. Questions immediately arose as to why he survived the crash while the other two did not. There were vicious rumours alleging that it was Ghazali, a licenced private pilot, who had been helming the plane, and that he had surrendered control to Vergis when it was too late to avoid a crash.

A source close to the case said: "One rumour is that there was a foreign woman inside the plane who should not have been there. It was also speculated that the Orang Asli found him that night and they took King Ghaz and hid him inside a cave. One of the pilot's friends told me that Ghaz wanted to get a better view of the mountains and flew too close and lost control."

Ghazali Shafie was a larger than life figure, having served under four prime ministers and participated in many important moments involving the country's history. He was, in fact, part of the Cobbold Commission that recommended the formation of Malaysia.

He served as home minister for much of the 1970s, emerging with great credit following his role as a negotiator during a hostage crisis in August 1975, when members of the Japanese Red Army terrorist organisation stormed the AIA building on Jalan Ampang, Kuala Lumpur and took more than 50 hostages. He got rather less approval though for a string of ISA detentions during his tenure, particularly in the aftermath of the 1974 Baling farmers' rights demonstrations.

A lengthy inquest was held, concluding a full 17 months after the crash. On June 22, 1983, the coroner Abdullah Sidek returned a verdict of death due to accident. Pulling no punches he declared: "I am of the opinion that being the pilot in command (then) Ghazali was directly responsible for the crash as he had final authority as to the disposition of the aircraft before the crash."

He said Ghazali was negligent in allowing the aircraft to proceed through the Waterworks Gap, knowing that the cloud and the cloud base were too low and neither of the pilots was instrument-rated (qualified to fly through clouds using instruments in low visibility). Abdullah also wrote that: "It has been amply proved that Ghazali Shafie was the pilot in command of the aircraft at all material times before the crash. He was seated on the left hand side of the cockpit."

Eddie Chua has also attempted to crack the case, to no avail. "King Ghaz was a fascinating man. Some say he was closely linked to British Secret Services in fact. There is even an unverified story that there is an elite club in London for former MI-5 operatives and if you go there you will see his name on a plaque on the wall. What is certain is that at his peak he was a very powerful man, but somehow the top post eluded him and after the plane crash his power waned."

More than a decade after the accident, Martin Vengadesan was to meet Ghazali who was then enjoying semi-retirement. He was visiting Dakar, Senegal, where Martin's father was serving as the Malaysian ambassador. Over the course of an unforgettable three hours (and a few glasses of whisky), Ghazali revealed himself to be a master raconteur, regaling tales of the glory days when he was one of the most powerful men in Malaysia.

Ghazali was the only survivor of the crash. *The Star* file image (courtesy of Star Media Group).

However, when briefly alluding to the crash, his boisterous tone changed, and he spoke wistfully of a moment that he considered a fateful brush with death. Naturally he was not in a position to be questioned further; in fact, he seemed at times to be talking to himself. He offered no explanation, yet was clearly contrite. Ghazali passed away in 2010, and the full truth of what happened in the jungles of Pahang has passed with him.

VERDICT That Ghazali was the pilot of the crashed plane is in no doubt. Why he was the sole survivor of the crash will forever remain a mystery.

15

AN HONOUR KILLING

Date : April 14, 1982
Crime : An Umno politician is found murdered and a fast-rising
minister is accused of the crime

Details: It's hard to believe now but in 1982, the Mahathir-
Musa (Hitam) Cabinet promised to usher in a new period
of liberalisation and development. In the early 1980s long-
time ISA detainees were freed and a batch of fresh new
faces promised a bright future. One of the brightest stars
was Culture, Youth and Sports Minister Mokhtar Hashim,
who was already being spoken of as a future prime minister.

It all came crashing down in the run-up to the 1982
General Elections when the state assemblyman for
Gemencheh, Negeri Sembilan, Mohd Taha Talib was found
shot dead. A local heavyweight, he was Negeri Sembilan
State Assembly Speaker and his death was a huge shock. It
wasn't long before rumours seemed to implicate another
political strongman.

PK Katharason remembered the buzz at the time. "I

Mokhtar Hashim headed to court. *The Star* file image (courtesy of Star Media Group).

was with Mahathir at a press conference in Mulu, Sarawak when word came from IGP Hanif Omar that Taha had been murdered. Even then the news spread that a minister might have killed him.

"I also remember when Mokhtar was arrested three months later. He was staying at Section 16, PJ and the press got wind of it. We raced to his house, but he had left the place. They caught him at a roadblock."

What followed was a sensational trial. It was rare enough to see a Cabinet minister in the dock, what more charged with the murder of a fellow politician, under the Essential (Security Cases) Regulations 1975, which carries a mandatory death sentence.

Initially, he was charged at the Tampin Magistrate's Court but the case was transferred to the High Court in Kuala Lumpur. A marathon 75-day trial ensued, the longest criminal trial in Malaysia's history. The 31 witnesses called by the Prosecution were actually outnumbered by 43 defence witnesses!

Mokhtar was not the only man charged with Taha's murder. Charged along with him were village headman Rahmat Satiman, Nordin Johan, Aziz Abdullah and Aziz Tumpuk. At first Mokhtar was staunchly defended, with witnesses claiming that he was with them at the time of the crime, but slowly cracks began to appear in the defence.

But what on earth could possibly make a fast-rising politician gun down a fellow elected official? The first rumour to emerge was that it was a crime of passion. Taha was said to have been carrying on with someone close to Mokhtar. But other sources said the rivalry was even more deep-rooted.

PK Katharason said: "It was a long case. I remember that they said Mokhtar had used a pistol from Negeri. We knew that some ministers like Megat Junid carried guns, but I wouldn't have expected Mokhtar to be a killer. I remember him as a very cool man. What I heard was it was about more than just a personal grudge.

"You mustn't forget that Taha was assemblyman for Gemencheh which was in the Tampin constituency where Mokhtar was the MP. But while Mokhtar was fast-rising nationally, Taha had a well-organised following. Locally he had more support. During the election campaign something happened. They were two big fish fighting over the spoils in a small lake."

After the long trial, Mokhtar was found guilty and was sentenced to death along with Rahmat Satiman. Nordin

Johan and Aziz Abdullah were released without their defence being called, while Aziz Tumpuk passed away while awaiting trial. Rahmat Satiman won an appeal and was acquitted and discharged on July 23, 1983.

Mokhtar's death sentence was later commuted to life imprisonment in 1984 and after nearly nine years behind bars, he received a Royal Pardon from the Yang di-Pertuan Agong Sultan Azlan Shah. He has since melted away into obscurity, living a quiet life far removed from the promise of what might have been.

VERDICT Mokhtar Hashim was found guilty but was eventually pardoned.

16

ALL ABOUT THE MONEY

Date : July 18, 1983
Crime : A Bumiputra Finance Berhad bank official is sent to
investigate irregular transactions and winds up dead

Details: The 1970s saw rapid growth in the Malaysian economy as oil discoveries were allied to the robust traditional tin and rubber markets. The banking sector grew accordingly but the first major sign of trouble occurred in 1982 when a Hong Kong-based, Malaysian-owned company called the Carrian Group went into liquidation. Formed by one George Tan Soon Gin it had expanded rapidly but crashed suddenly.

It was then revealed that Bumiputra Finance Berhad (BMF) had authorised a massive RM2.5 billion in loans to the group. BMF was the subsidiary of Bank Bumiputra Malaysia Berhad. Jalil Ibrahim, a BMF assistant general manager, was sent to Hong Kong to investigate how the loans were approved.

A keen auditor, Jalil was perturbed by what he found

BMF investigator Jalil Ibrahim.

and made a classified report to his superiors in Malaysia upon a brief return for the Raya celebrations. He then went to Hong Kong a second time, only to be called out to a mysterious meeting. He told his staff he was going to meet an important man at Regent Hotel and was never seen alive again.

The next day, Jalil's body was discovered in a banana grove at Taipo Kau village in the rural New Territories district. The autopsy and police investigations revealed that Jalil had been strangled with a white bathrobe belt. His body was stuffed into a large suitcase, carted through the Regent Hotel lobby and loaded into a taxi before it was dumped. Incidentally at that time, Carrian owned Hong Kong's largest taxi company.

Jalil's killing provoked an uproar both in Malaysia and Hong Kong. Rumours linked various politicians and financiers to the scandal. Soon another Malaysian Mak

Foon Than was arrested and charged with his murder. Mak was found guilty by the Hong Kong High Court.

A source who remembers the case said: "At that time it was really complicated. Malaysia was a young country enjoying newfound wealth but suddenly you had all these murders and conspiracies. The sums of money being thrown about were enormous then. In a way it was every bit as scandalous back then as the 1Malaysia Development Berhad corruption cases have become for the present generation.

"In retrospect, it seems clear that Jalil was an honest man about to uncover a huge can of worms and some people would stop at nothing, even murder, to cover their tracks.

"During the trial, all kinds of things came out. Bank staff were asked to shred documents, the henchman pointed the finger at various unnamed VIPs, I think someone else close to the case on the Hong Kong side committed suicide. At one point even a juror was assaulted, threatening the trial."

While Mak appeared to have been the henchman, he clearly killed Jalil under orders. His wildly varying testimony indicated that he was hired by a Korean middleman and the killing was done on behalf of a very powerful and wealthy individual who may or may not have been Malaysian or Singaporean. Mak himself only ever admitted to having helped dispose of Jalil's body.

Jalil's tragic murder investigations by Hong Kong's Independent Commission Against Corruption took many years (effectively from 1983 to 2000). At the centre of it was George Tan, who escaped significant jail time despite going to trial on a number of occasions. Other individuals, including then BMF Chairman Lorrain Esme Osman, were also implicated in the financial aspects. He was arrested in London in December 1985 but fought lengthy extradition battles, eventually serving a year in jail in the early 1990s after pleading guilty to a count of financial negligence.

VERDICT Jalil's murder has not truly been solved as the real brains behind his killing has not been brought to justice.

17

THE UNEXPLAINED RAMPAGE

Date : October 18, 1987
Crime : A soldier runs amok in the heart of Kuala Lumpur, triggering panic and a political crisis

Details: This is a particularly tricky case to describe because it draws in a fair number of disparate threads, not all of which can be discussed openly yet. Superficially, the scene begins with a soldier Private Adam Jaafar who took leave of his senses. In possession of an M-16, he showed up at Kuala Lumpur's Chow Kit district and randomly opened fire causing fatal injuries.

The incident provoked fears of another round of racial riots that might emulate the terrors of May 13, 1969. Within days of this rampage, more than 100 prominent personalities were detained under the Internal Security Act under the infamous *Operation Lalang. The Star* newspaper was also gagged, ushering in a period of political repression.

Michael Chong has a vivid recollection of when news of the shooting broke. "During this time there was chaos. People feared another May 13. All the sundry shops quickly ran out of provisions. I remember I was having Hokkien mee at a restaurant in Jalan 222, PJ, when I got the call. I was told something serious is happening and there might be racial killings. So many people walked off during dinner. I also quickly walked off without paying the bill!

"After a while the mood calmed down very quickly. The reason for this is that the shooter was Malay and the victim also was Malay. If the victim had been Chinese then there might have been an increase of tension and fear, but because she was not, the situation didn't actually get so heated."

However, details began to surface about Adam's background and the reason for his tragic and violent breakdown. Adam, a ranger, had failed to turn up for weapons training camp at Jalan Tambun, Ipoh. Instead he went AWOL with his weapon and surfaced in Kuala Lumpur where he began shooting indiscriminately.

Why did Adam do what he did? Two vastly differing stories emerged. The first was of a young man who snapped after being viciously bullied in camp. It was said that he was beaten and forced to perform oral sex on his seniors. His only escape was his fondness and skill for shooting and when practice was cancelled, he snapped. The story told in court depicted a tragic life of a man who had had a number of serious head injuries and who witnessed his sister dying in a fire right before his eyes.

Apparently, Adam had intended to shoot at buildings, not people. He had in fact scrawled a suicide note of sorts on the mirror of his hotel room. It read '*Malam sial untuk Adam. Membunuh, dibunuh atau bunuh diri*'. Literally it read: 'It is a cursed night for Adam. To kill or be killed or to kill myself.'

The other story that was kept out of the courts and the newspapers was somewhat different. It was rumoured that Adam was distraught because his brother had died under harrowing circumstances, allegedly at the hands of one of the country's most powerful men.

Given the 'sensitivity' of the situation, much of the truth was kept from the Malaysian public and many were not keen to be quoted on the subject. Filmmaker Amir Muhammad tackled the incident in his 2003 film *The Big Durian* but perhaps ultimately left us with more questions than answers.

More light was shed on the matter in 2017, when a book entitled *The Confessions of Private Adam* was released. In it, he says that there was no connection whatsoever with powerful royals, and no truth to the rumour that his brother was killed while serving as a caddy to a public figure. "Every time I was interrogated, they tried to link my fate to royalty," Adam said. He added that he finally gave in and implicated others, but that there was no conspiracy whatsoever.

"They alleged that individuals were behind my action in a bid to divert public attention away from the problems that were plaguing the Malaysian leadership at that time," the book quotes Adam as saying.

In April 2018, Adam's younger sister Hawa Jaafar denied the urban legend saying the family had to hold back their shame and anger for 30 years because they were unable to explain the truth to the public and the authorities.

"Adam went amok in Chow Kit due to problems in his workplace and not because our brother was killed by the Sultan. I want to clarify that there were no deaths involving our siblings due to murder. All of us are still alive except for one who passed away in 1975 in a fire," she said.

VERDICT Adam Jaafar was found not guilty by reason of temporary insanity. He spent many years in a mental institution but was eventually freed.

18

BRUTALISED BABY BALA

Date : May 13, 1990
Crime : A toddler is brutally tortured and dumped like garbage
in a hospital toilet

Details: In 1990, a two-year-old boy was found abandoned in the Kuala Lumpur Hospital. He had been dumped like garbage in the hospital toilet, beaten until virtually comatose. It was a small flicker of movement that led to his being scooped up and cared for by horrified hospital staff.

His little body was full of scars and cigarette burns and he had suffered massive internal injuries. The poor baby fought for his life for another 48 hours in the Intensive Care Unit, but eventually succumbed. His injuries were so severe that even the best efforts by his doctors could not save him from death.

When he died, not even his name B Balasundram was known. Eventually, the story emerged of how this adorable little child was tortured to death over a few weeks in a

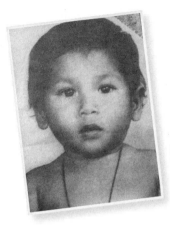

Newspaper clipping of the late Baby Bala. *The Star* file image (courtesy of Star Media Group).

back room in Chow Kit, Kuala Lumpur, between April and May 1990.

The two-year-old was born to young parents. His mother K Kaliamah was only 16 when he was born and worked as a prostitute, while his truck driver father languished in jail. Bala's mother left him in the care of a Madam, identified variously as Madam Maliga or S Chellamah, but did not return to pick him up as promised.

Unfortunately for Bala, Chellamah also lived with a drug addict K Sinnasamy. Sinnasamy objected to the boy's presence and beat him mercilessly whenever he committed an infraction, perceived or otherwise. Bala soon became shy and withdrawn, and his face and body became full of bruises and welts.

After a few weeks of being beaten, kicked and eventually burnt and sodomised by Sinnasamy, Bala's body succumbed. He was unable to walk, and Sinnasamy said that he would take him to the nearby General Hospital to be checked. Instead, Sinnasamy took Bala to the hospital and proceeded to dump him in the toilets.

When discussing this tragedy, both the late Karpal Singh and Martin Vengadesan became emotional and teared up. "It was the worst case I have ever witnessed in 40 years of practising law," Karpal said in 2012. "I've never seen such cruelty. What was done to that boy was unforgivable and then to leave him to die like that. It was horrible. All my life I have been a staunch opponent of the death penalty but I think when a child has been raped, tortured and murdered, and there is clearly a guilty party with no room for doubt, then I'm all for it.

"To be fair, the Barisan Nasional government has done all it can. It has recognised the problem, set up helplines, introduced the right laws and been proactive to fight this social evil. But this sort of crime often happens behind closed doors with a helpless victim, and by the time we find out, it's usually too late. Of course, it's no excuse but most of the time the abuser was himself abused as a child."

We asked Malaysia Mental Health Association (MMHA) president Dr Andrew Mohanraj whether most abusers had themselves been victims in the past. But it turns out it's not so simple.

"An abuser may have been an abuse victim in the past (childhood), but it's not true in most cases actually," he said.

"In cases of anti-social personality disorder, severe depression or even in certain psychotic disorders, the abusers need not have been victims themselves.

"However, it is true that severe childhood trauma can result in the abused becoming the abuser in adulthood. There are many theories for this, but one that is commonly subscribed to is that the child associates abuse with power and the victim as being powerless and vulnerable.

"Sadly, when the child becomes an adult, to feel secure and powerful he associates abuse in the form of anger bursts or bullying as a form of maintaining power, and fears becoming the victim again.

"Displacement of anger is a vicious cycle that requires retrospection and understanding and coming to terms with one's own limitations and embracing one's own strengths to break this cycle."

Whatever his reasoning, Sinnasamy was found guilty on May 7, 1992, and sentenced to hang for Bala's murder. He had protested during the trial that a confession was beaten out of him while he was suffering from narcotics withdrawal.

Gallingly in 1999, Sinnasamy had his death sentence commuted to 20 years in prison and 10 strokes of the rotan, which means he was released some years ago.

VERDICT A cruel killer was found guilty but had his sentence commuted and now he is free to live a life he brutally denied Baby Bala. Bala's tragic death led to the passing of the Child Protection Act 1991.

19

THE BENTONG KALI SPREE

Date : June 29, 1993
Crime : A notorious gang leader dies in a shootout in
an affluent neighbourhood

Details: Not to be confused with the similarly-named Batang Kali, Bentong Kali was the nickname of P Kalimuthu, a ruthless killer who hailed from the town of Bentong, Pahang. A life-long gangster, Bentong Kali gained notoriety in the early 1990s when he began killing with increasing frequency and callousness. When his crime spree prompted a police offensive, it all ended in a bloody shootout during which Bentong Kali was killed.

Born in 1961, Bentong Kali dropped out of school at the age of 14 and soon drifted into the company of the Chinese secret societies. For many years he was in and out of prison, serving his first term in 1980, when he was 19 and experiencing a spell of restricted residence in Kuantan, Pahang in 1987. When he wasn't behind bars, he 'built his name' in the 08 and 04 gangs which were involved in

Ruthless killer, Bentong Kali.

extortion and armed robbery.

Heavily tattooed and with a burgeoning reputation for indiscriminate violence, Bentong Kali became a national figure in the early 1990s when he took his criminal activities 'above ground'. During this time, he was actually caught twice in quick succession. In April 1990, he was detained during a drug raid but freed due to lack of evidence. He was subsequently arrested in January 1991 and placed under another spell of restricted residence, this time in Gopeng, Perak. Later in 1991, he went to Petaling Jaya, Selangor to attend a court hearing and took the chance to escape from detention.

By this time all bets were off, and Bentong Kali and his gang were linked to no less than 17 murders in less than two years. Among them included six killings at a wedding dinner in Sungai Petani, Kedah, the shooting of a Royal Malaysian Air Force civilian staff and many targeted killings of other hoodlums who had crossed his path.

Bentong Kali grew increasingly daring, using the same gun for his killings, and often using a motorcycle for swift drive-by shootings. When he heard that the famed policeman,

Criminal Investigation Department Director Zaman Khan had been put in charge of a task force to apprehend him, he cheekily called the latter and taunted him.

Veteran crime reporter Andrew Sagayam said: "Bentong Kali is believed to have called up Zaman saying things like 'you can't catch me', and he even told him 'some of your policemen are actually working under me'. That made Zaman all the more determined to catch him.

"One thing clear about Bentong Kali is that he used to admire Botak Chin and there are quite a few parallels because Bentong Kali was imitating him all along. He started by extorting his classmates, moved his way up the gang ladder, and because he was in a small town like Bentong, he had a big impact. But later he became greedy and reckless."

Eddie Chua said: "Bentong Kali was yet another one of those sensationalist characters. Yes, he was a gangster but he also enjoyed the publicity I think. Somebody once showed me a video of Bentong Kali courting his girlfriend. There was the fella singing Hindi songs while sitting on a swing. This is a side of him that no one could imagine!"

Living on the run and relying on a network of trusted friends, Bentong Kali did indeed try to cultivate the folk hero status that Botak Chin had enjoyed two decades earlier. But on June 29, 1993, time ran out for him.

Sagayam said: "On the night before he was shot, Bentong Kali went out drinking in a very public place, especially when you consider there was a manhunt for him and a bounty of RM100,000 offered for information leading to his capture. He went to Street Connections in

Damansara Heights. What he didn't know was that the police had gotten one of his gang members to lure him to the area. After drinking, that member left, saying that he was going to set up a business meeting for Bentong Kali in a house nearby."

That was how Bentong Kali and two trusted lieutenants ended up cornered in a house on Medan Damansara. Despite being surrounded by Special Action Squad members, Bentong Kali and his gang members tried to shoot their way out. Bentong Kali was killed almost instantly through a shot to the head, and his murderous spree was brought to a screeching halt.

Bentong Kali's body being removed after the shootout. *The Star* file image (courtesy of Star Media Group).

VERDICT Bentong Kali was a ruthless killer who led a charmed life. His reckless style meant that he was bound to meet a violent death.

20

POP SINGER, WITCH DOCTOR

Date : July 2, 1993
Crime : Rising politician Mazlan Idris is found dead, with
former singer Mona Fandey accused of the crime

Details: The grisly murder of Umno politician Mazlan
Idris in 1993 was a case that forced many Malaysians
to acknowledge their superstitious side. Here was
Mazlan, a US-educated politician and assemblyman
for Batu Talam, Pahang, who was extremely wealthy
and successful. Yet he was willing to trade large sums
of money for further glory and riches, and ultimately
ended up trading his life.

That his killing was carried out on the orders of a witch-
like *bomoh* (witch doctor) known as Mona Fandey only
served to draw more attention to the case. Mona Fandey had
a ghastly, gothic appearance that somehow called to mind
supernatural creatures from local myths, most notably the
pontianak, a vampire-like female ghost with a pale face and
long dark hair. Many found themselves irresistibly drawn to

the case, and still shudder with revulsion at the mention of Mona's 'exploits'.

More straightforwardly, Mona was just a homicidal con artist. Born Maznah Ismail in Perlis in 1956, she was believed to have Thai blood which, rightly or wrongly, tends to be associated with the witch doctor trade. However, that was not the first path she attempted to tread. She initially tried to make it as a sultry crooner recording under the name of Maznah Ismail. Her self-financed album *Diana 1* and attendant singles *Ku Nyanyikan Lagu Ini* and *Ratapan Anak* hardly made any waves, but her television appearances performing them now make for fascinating viewing on YouTube.

The underwhelming response to her pipes persuaded Mona to try a different line and she decided to make the transition to dabbling in black magic. She teamed up with her husband Mohamad Affandi Abdul Rahman and soon discovered that superstition was a lucrative business, as many important people were prepared to pay exorbitant sums of money for a promise of supernatural aid.

Mazlan was one such client. When told that Mona and her husband could give him some talismans that had belonged to the late Indonesian President Sukarno, Mazlan paid RM500,000 and transferred land worth RM2 million to Mona. While that begs the question of where the politician was able to obtain such wealth, it was soon to lead to something more sinister.

Naturally enough, the time came for Mona to deliver on these wild promises. That Mona's method was rooted in

Mona Fandey being brought to court. *The Star* file image (courtesy of Star Media Group).

madness soon emerged when she carried out a cleansing ritual for Mazlan. The unsuspecting politician came to Mona's house and was asked to lie down while he was covered in flowers. He was apparently told to close his eyes and wait for money to fall from the sky. What actually fell was the axe of Mona's assistant, Juraimi Hassan!

After three hacks, Mazlan was beheaded. The gruesome ordeal didn't end there as Mona, Affandi and Juraimi proceeded to dismember the body, chopping it up into 18 pieces!

Rather than disappear with their ill-gotten gains, Mona and her hubby decided to indulge themselves. She bought a Mercedes Benz and reportedly underwent some plastic surgery. Given that Mazlan had been reported missing for more than two weeks prior to his death, and he was an elected official, this was surely a red flag to the authorities.

Sure enough, within days of the murder, the police raided Mona's house, finding traces of Mazlan's body. Amazingly, when the case went to trial at Temerloh High Court, Mona actually had a bevy of well-wishers and curious onlookers to 'perform' to. She seemed to derive great pleasure from all the attention, waving to the press and the public, and taking good care to put on a fashion show of gaudy outfits.

Andrew Sagayam said: "While the trial was going on, it was rumoured that Mona Fandey was causing havoc in the lock-up. It was said that she was seen floating around and muttering supernatural spells. Then apparently when she was handcuffed, she just removed them like bangles. The word is that the lawyers and police had to go in with three or four *bomohs* of their own just to counter her power!"

The trial itself was relatively swift and straightforward, although both Affandi and Juraimi came across as blind followers of the scheming Mona. It was one of the last trials before the jury system was abolished and all three were duly found guilty and sentenced to death. However, there were Federal Court appeals and yet another round of legal wrangling when the trio tried to get a last-minute pardon. On each of these occasions, Mona played to the gallery. However, there was one time when she was shocked to find merely a miniscule crowd as she emerged from a Black Maria.

Eventually, more than eight years after Mazlan's murder, Mona, Affandi and Juraimi were hanged on

November 2, 2001, in Kajang Prison. It is said that just before her execution, Mona smiled calmly and said, "I will never die."

Eddie Chua was there. "It was the last thing that she said just before she died. I can't forget her saying that just before she went to the gallows. She said, 'I will live forever.' People from around the world called me about that."

As it turned out, Mona's words were swiftly proven to be as false as every other claim she had made.

Yet, for all her blatant chicanery, Mona Fandey continued to attract attention from beyond the grave. Two notable filmmakers addressed her story, Amir Muhammad with *Mona* (2002) and Dain Said with the fictionalised *Dukun* (2006), although the latter movie was released a full 12 years after its initial completion due to legal and censorship issues.

VERDICT Mona, Affandi and Juraimi were found guilty and hanged eight years after their heinous crime.

21

A MINOR OFFENCE

Date : August 1994
Crime : An underaged girl admits to sexual intercourse with
a number of men, allegedly naming a prominent public
figure among them

Details: Back in the mid-1990s, the government started
getting serious about what it termed the 'bohsia'
phenomenon. This referred to what was considered to
be promiscuity among teenage girls. In a sensational
development, a teenager in Melaka was held in protective
custody after 'confessing' to having had sexual intercourse
with 15 men. This already sensational case garnered even
more attention because one of the names she cited was one
of the most prominent personalities of the time.

The girl's grandmother sought the aid of prominent
DAP officials to act on her behalf. She claimed that the
girl was being detained by police, ostensibly for her own
protection but without parental consent, while they
investigated the case. The girl's name was actually revealed

Lim Guan Eng arrested. *The Star* file image (courtesy of Star Media Group).

but as she was a minor at the time, her name shall remain anonymous in this account.

Then Kota Melaka MP Lim Guan Eng was foremost among those who took up her case. He was outraged when charges were brought against the other men alleged to have had sex with the girl while the 'big gun' was not charged due to a lack of evidence. Lim began a campaign to protest this decision but, in a strange twist of fate, found himself in the dock instead!

On February 28, 1995, he was accused under the Sedition Act of prompting 'disaffection with the administration of justice in Malaysia' for having stated that 'double standards' were being applied by the Attorney General Mohtar

Abdullah in this case. He was also charged with maliciously printing a pamphlet containing false information because the pamphlet had described the girl as an 'imprisoned victim'.

What followed was another lengthy trial and appeal process. Lim was found guilty and sentenced on April 28, 1997, to two fines amounting to RM15,000. The Attorney General appealed against this sentence and after a number of appeals, Lim was sentenced to two concurrent 18-month prison terms in August 1998.

Ironically, in December 1998, the girl emerged to tell a press conference that her allegations of having had intimate relations with the politician were fabricated and that she was forced to lie to the police in 1994. Her angry grandmother then held a counter press conference refuting this turnaround and chastising her granddaughter for it.

A source close to the case recalled: "This was a very tough time for Guan Eng. I remember his father Kit Siang himself breaking down in tears when Guan Eng was hauled off to jail. At the same time, it played a crucial part in establishing Guan Eng's credentials. There were those among the Malay community who felt that an injustice was being carried out, and they were touched and ashamed that Guan Eng was going to prison for defending the girl when others were standing idly by."

The young girl in the case eventually assumed a life of anonymity, settling down and getting married. Lim was released after serving 12 months, his sentenced reduced for good behaviour. He was barred from contesting in elections for five years, but made a stunning comeback in 2008, served a decade as Penang Chief Minister, before becoming Malaysia's Finance Minister in 2018.

VERDICT Today the girl has returned to normal life, while the key political actors are still active.

22

GANGS FOR THE MEMORIES

Date : August 31, 1994
Crime : A gang breaks into an airport cargo hold and makes off
with RM12 million in gold bars, marking the start of a
decade of prominent gang heists

Details: On Merdeka Day in 1994, a Malaysian Airlines
cargo terminal in the recently 'retired' Subang Airport was
broken into. The nation was shocked to learn that a well-
organised armed gang of criminals had made off with 300
gold bars worth RM12 million. The heist was soon revealed
to be the work of the Mamak gang. As years passed, other
gangs such as the Steyr gang and the M-16 gang also
became equally notorious.

The Mamak gang had apparently started off as a
small gang of brothers from Kuala Kangsar, Perak, who
concentrated their operations on warehouse ambushes.
One of its key trademarks was that a gang member would
dress up as a policeman and assume a position of authority,
making it easy for them to execute their crime.

Mohd Yusof Abu Bakar, founding member of the Mamak Gang.

By the late 1990s, however, the Mamak gang activity had died down. It was around this time that the Steyr gang surfaced. Known to have a number of former army commandos amongst their ranks, the Steyr gang enjoyed a brief and violent spell in the limelight. Between August 1999 and January 2000, they committed around 10 robberies, targeting banks and jewellery stores. Armed with powerful Steyr AUG assault rifles which they had taken in a daring raid on Royal Ordnance Corps in Kamunting, Perak, their spree ended when four gang members were shot dead by police in shootouts in Johor.

There was no time for the police to rest, however, because less than a month later, the M-16 gang began an even more daring run of robberies. In a two-year period that ended in late 2002, the M-16 gang pulled off a series of slick high-profile robberies, often employing the same tactics. They would be well-armed with M-16s, wear ski masks, descend upon the target area with a unit of eight to

10 members and carry out their attack with swift precision.

Unlike the two previous gangs, the M-16 members were known for speaking Cantonese and being particularly smooth as their attacks hardly involved any actual violence or loss of life. It is believed that in more than 15 robberies over a two-year period, the M-16 gang bagged over RM20 million in cash and jewellery.

Beginning with a RM500,000 robbery at a pawn shop in Pudu in January 2000, their famous heists included a RM2 million hit on two goldsmith shops in Sungai Buloh (August 9, 2000), a RM3 million operation at a jewellery store in Seremban (December 26, 2000), a RM2 million robbery at Endah Parade, Seri Petaling just two days later (December 28, 2000), two separate million-dollar hits in Johor in mid to late 2001 and a RM500,000 attack on jewellers on Jalan Tuanku Abdul Rahman, Kuala Lumpur (December 17, 2001).

Unlike the Mamak and Steyr gangs, there did not appear to be a violent end to the M-16 gang's activities. In fact, it was almost as if the gang members decided they had made enough and closed down. Remnants of the Mamak gang, however, were active for much longer, with a series of important arrests made in December 2006, and a fatal shootout in 2008.

Andrew Sagayam covered crimes committed by all three gangs. He said: "It is very clear from day one, that all these gangs contained disgruntled ex-police and ex-army personnel. The Mamak gang probably had more of an ex-police link, while the Steyr and M-16 gangs were more military in nature. While there are obviously some technical differences, I am convinced that all three gangs have some connection.

"What they had in common was access to high-powered firearms and uniforms that were so convincing members of the public would never challenge them. These were rolling operations, meaning when some members got caught or were otherwise put out of commission, there were others to take their place. In fact, there were times when the gangs were being run by guys who were actually detained under Restricted Residence and Emergency Orders!"

Eddie Chua also actively covered the three gangs. "When it comes to the Mamak gang, I actually interviewed the original mamak himself, one of the Abu Bakar brothers. Can you imagine? I didn't even have his number. I just drove to his place in Perak and knocked on his door. And he welcomed me in and talked to me!

"By then he had done his time, and served a few years under the Emergency Ordinance. He said that he had committed crimes and done his sentence, but that after him many used the name the Mamak gang but actually had nothing to do with him or his original gang."

Chua also courted some controversy himself by interviewing a suspect on the run. "I nearly got into trouble with the M-16 case because I got a tip-off from a contact and I ended up interviewing the suspect before he was arrested! These gangs had many links to the military and the police. He was a former weapons expert from one of the Singapore special forces and he could dismantle and put together rifles and revolvers within a few seconds. Eventually, he was not arrested but caught in a shootout and killed."

Sagayam believes there is a specific reason why the identities of the gang members have been kept so quiet. "We know some stories about them, that the Mamak gang was started by a pair of Indian-Muslim brothers, and that the M-16 gang is believed to have been mainly Chinese, but the names are rarely if ever released to the public. I think one of the reasons is because their identities would be embarrassing to the police and the army. It was also obvious from the efficiency of their operations and their ability to make clean escapes that the gangs had inside information from within the police force.

"Notably there was not much overlap between the activity of the three gangs. The M-16 in particular ran very smooth operations. There was not much killing or violence in their crimes and when I spoke to witnesses and victims, they said it was just like a scene from the movies ... a professional job executed by men in ski masks who moved in commando-like specific formations.

"I was also told that the recruitment for these gangs was also top notch. The leaders didn't just pick any old thug. You needed to be reliable and well-trained, as well as be personally trustworthy and loyal to the gang. That's why these gangs were able to do so much damage and get away with it."

While there was never a concerted public prosecution of the aforementioned gangs per se, there was a well-publicised attempt to crack down on the growing influence of criminal gangs in 2013, when top cops named specific gangs such as Gang 04, Gang 24 and Gang 36. In 2017 and 2018, there was an increase in arrests such as that of a 'Datuk Seri' who led Gang 77 in July 2017. The Ops Cantas operation that was held at the time brought in some 70 suspects in fact.

However, on December 17, 2017, a gang leader was dragged and stabbed by four suspects before he was run over twice in a petrol station in Johor, confirming that violent gangs are still well and truly alive.

The Mamak gang may have taken a backseat to these other gangs, but incarnations of the gang are clearly still active. On January 28, 2017, a Mamak gang founder with 26 criminal convictions fired several shots at police and was killed when they returned fire after a 10km high-speed chase from Setia Alam to Bukit Cherakah, Shah Alam. On May 22, 2018, another shootout in Rembau, Negeri Sembilan led to the deaths of two men in their early 30s. They were said by police to be remnants of the Mamak gang.

VERDICT Despite the high-profile nature of these crimes, most prominent gang members were never identified, arrested nor charged in court for the big heists.

23

A HOLE IN THE CASE

Date : September 1998
Crime : The Deputy Prime Minister Anwar Ibrahim is accused of sodomy, kicking off two decades of sex-related scandals

Details: Like a string of action movies with each instalment seeking to be more spectacular than the previous one, a series of sodomy trials and other sexual allegations have long dogged former deputy prime minister Anwar Ibrahim. The first trial came soon after his stunning dismissal from the Cabinet in September 1998.

The first indication of this scandal came when a book, *50 Dalil Kenapa Anwar Tidak Boleh Jadi PM* (50 Reasons Why Anwar Cannot Become Prime Minister), was put in circulation. Still, it was a massive shock when Anwar, the presumptive successor to Prime Minister Dr Mahathir Mohamad, was fired.

Worse was to follow when Anwar's former speechwriter Dr Munawar Anees and his adopted brother Sukma

Darmawan were arrested under suspicion of engaging in homosexual acts. Day after day, Anwar was hit with fresh accusations and insinuations as Ummi Hafilda Ali (sister of both television personality Azwan Ali and Anwar's then protege Azmin Ali) was revealed as a potential key witness. His driver, Azizan Abu Bakar, was also alleged to have been sodomised.

On September 29, 1998, Anwar himself was charged with corruption and sodomy. He was then pictured arriving at court with a black eye, which he claimed was the result of a beating from then Inspector-General of Police Rahim Noor. Despite some confusion over the validity of the confessions of Munawar and Sukma (with both men retracting their testimony at one point), the trial went ahead.

A mattress was infamously presented in court (in fact it was brought in and out on numerous occasions) which was alleged to have Anwar's semen stains and to be the site of his adulterous sodomy. To add to the controversy, it appeared as if the Prosecution alleged that an act of sodomy had occurred inside a building that was not even constructed at the time of the supposed event.

Despite all that, on April 14, 1999, Anwar was sentenced to six years in prison for corruption. On August 8, 2000, he received a further nine-year sentence for sodomy. In July 2002, Anwar lost his final appeal against the corruption conviction in the Federal Court.

However, once Dr Mahathir stepped down and was replaced by Abdullah Badawi, Anwar's fortunes in the courts improved. In September 2004, the Federal Court overturned his sodomy conviction and Anwar was freed from prison. Next, a Royal Commission was convened and Rahim Noor admitted that he had assaulted Anwar resulting in Anwar's infamous black eye. Rahim was eventually charged and given a two-month prison sentence.

Yet, Anwar's legal battles were far from over. Within months of his masterminding an electoral success on March 8, 2008, his aide Mohd Saiful Bukhari Azlan lodged a police report claiming that he had been sodomised by Anwar. This time, Anwar dramatically took refuge in the Turkish Embassy in Kuala Lumpur. On July 16, 2008, a huge contingent of police cars arrived at the embassy to arrest Anwar.

In his second trial, which began in earnest in February 2010, Anwar again faced controversial DNA samples. On this occasion, there was a dispute over the semen specimens found in Saiful's anal region and the length of their survival. Despite Saiful swearing on the Quran that he was sodomised, Anwar was eventually acquitted on January 12, 2012. All this occurred amidst much drama as three explosions went off outside the court.

By then, Anwar had yet another sex scandal to contend with! In March 2011, a mysterious trio, collectively known as Datuk T, screened a sex video to members of the media at Carcosa Seri Negara. The video allegedly featured a sex act involving someone resembling Anwar and a female prostitute. Soon, the Datuk T trio was revealed to be former Melaka chief minister Abdul Rahim Tamby Chik, businessman Shazryl Eskay Abdullah and Perkasa treasurer

Shuib Lazim. Despite much controversy and speculation, no criminal proceedings followed.

In March 2014, Anwar found himself back in court as the Court of Appeal judged that the High Court had failed to 'critically evaluate' the evidence submitted by the government chemist who testified. They overturned his acquittal and sentenced him to five years in jail. On February 10, 2015, the Federal Court of Malaysia upheld that decision and Anwar, by then nearly 68 years old, was sent back to jail.

Finally, after the general election of May 9, 2018, Anwar's Parti Keadilan Rakyat was part of the triumphant Pakatan Harapan coalition (ironically led by a returning Mahathir) and Anwar was granted a pardon on May 14, 2018. His most recent spell in jail saw him weakened in health. Anwar's detention as a student leader from 1974 to 1976 and his two stints in jail after the sodomy and corruption trials meant that he had spent a decade of his life behind bars.

VERDICT Through all the scandalous trials and allegations, it was clear that Anwar was being tried for reasons that were more about politics than the committing of any crime.

24

CULT SEIZES ARMY CAMP

Date : July 2, 2000
Crime : A terrorist cult steals arms from a military base and calls for a coup

Details: The Persaudaraan Ilmu Dalam Al-Ma'unah (Brotherhood of Al-Ma'unah Inner Power) was a terrorist group with extreme religious and political beliefs. Known simply as Al-Ma'unah, the group created national headlines when they carried out a daring raid on a Malaysian Army Reserve camp in Gerik, Perak on July 2, 2000.

Led by a fanatical ex-army private Mohamed Amin Mohamed Razali, Al-Ma'unah stole weapons from the armoury and holed themselves up with some hostages in the nearby village of Sauk. Eventually, a standoff against the Malaysian army and police ended in the capture of the group, but not before two military personnel and a militant were killed.

Andrew Sagayam said: "I think they were a deviant group, but not all of Amin's followers were religious guys.

Many were just angry with the government and authority in general. In fact some of the Steyr gang members were found to be involved in Al-Ma'unah.

"The manner in which they conned their way into the 304th Malaysian Army Reserve (Rejimen Askar Wataniah) camp was very similar to what the Mamak gang and the Steyr gang used to do. They impersonated officers, wearing uniforms that were similar, and they even had a forged letter from the Ministry of Defence, but using the real letterhead!"

Indeed, Al-Ma'unah personnel did dress up as senior military officers and arrive at the reserve camp in three well-disguised Pajeros. They pretended it was a surprise inspection and took possession of much of the weaponry and communications there. By the time they got to Sauk, Al-Ma'unah had taken hostages with them.

They then issued a demand that they would besiege Kuala Lumpur if Prime Minister Dr Mahathir Mohamad did not resign within 24 hours. Amin also despatched some members to bomb the Anchor and Carlsberg breweries in Petaling Jaya and the Hindu temple in Batu Caves, although only minimal damage was inflicted.

The hostages were police personnel Sergeant Mohd Shah Ahmad and Detective Corporal Sanghadevan as well as civilian Jaafar Puteh who had, unfortunately, wandered into the camp while looking for durians! Later, army trooper Matthews Medan was also captured. Sadly, it was later revealed during the trial that Amin and his men had brutally tortured Matthews and Sanghadevan, both

Al-Ma'unah founder Mohd Amin. *The Star* file image (courtesy of Star
Media Group).

of whom were killed. They had allegedly been targeted
because they were non-Muslims.

After a three-day siege, during which time the militants
were surrounded by a joint team of army and police special
forces, Amin and his men finally agreed to surrender.
During the surrender, however, Amin lost his cool and
attempted to shoot the Malaysian Army Field Commander,
Lieutenant General Zaini Mohamad Said at point blank
range. Zaini flicked the gun and Amin's shot killed his own
man, Abdul Halim Ali.

Amin and his followers were later brought to trial on
the charge of waging war upon the King. He and two
of his lieutenants, Zahit Muslim and Jamaluddin, were
sentenced to death as was cult member, Jemari Jusoh,
who had executed Matthews. A further 16 other members
were given life sentences. Amin was eventually hanged on

August 4, 2006, a week after Zahit, Jamaluddin and Jemari were executed.

Professor Shamsul Amri said: "These groups will emerge in every society. You have those within the mainstream of society and others who are marginalised from mainstream development. Then there are still others who are so alienated that they seek to build up their society with its own rules and its own promises. They can be very disciplined because they are fanatically devoted. If motivated by religion or nationalism, they can feel aggrieved that their belief is not accepted by all.

"We see extreme acts all the time. The Oklahoma bombings (April 19, 1995), the attacks on the World Trade Centre (September 11, 2001) and we saw it in Norway with this Anders Breivik's bombing and shooting (July 22, 2011) and up to 2019 with the terror attacks in Christchurch, New Zealand and Colombo, Sri Lanka. Can you imagine how devoted or deluded these men must have been to take such actions?

"There is usually a similar set of conditions that can result in such people being pushed to their limits and taking extreme action. They plot and plan to take over the world always. They don't have the means but they can do some damage.

"They will find a vehicle to express these desires for self-aggrandisement. The leader will take on messiah-like qualities in the eyes of his followers and they actually feel as if they are doing good even though they are committing murder or other cruel acts!"

The Al-Ma'unah incident was far from the first time groups mixing political and religious views came into conflict with the authorities, who viewed them as dangerous cults. During the Memali incident in Baling, Kedah, in 1985, there was a face-off between the police and supporters of Ibrahim Mahmud @ Ibrahim Libya.

On November 19, 1985, nearly 200 policemen laid siege to a group of around 400 of Ibrahim's fanatical followers. Working themselves up into a frenzied state, villagers charged the police resulting in the deaths of 14 civilians, including Ibrahim and four policemen.

Ibrahim Mahmud, who got his nickname after studying at the University of Tripoli in Libya, was a long-time political activist, twice contesting in general elections for the seat of Bayu-Baling under the PAS banner. However, he became increasingly radicalised and opposition to his teachings and attempts by the police to detain him led to the emotional and poorly-managed stand-off in Baling.

In 1994, the Al-Arqam movement was proscribed by the National Fatwa Council in August and banned by the federal government a few months later. Senior Al-Arqam leaders, including its head Ashaari Mohammad, were detained under the ISA amid claims that the 10,000-strong movement was founding its own army.

There was also the Sky Kingdom commune in Besut, Terengganu, which was destroyed in July 2005 by masked assailants acting in complicity with the authorities. Far from aiding members of the commune, the property was razed by officials of the Besut Land Office a couple of weeks after. The Sky Kingdom's founding father Ayah Pin fled into exile while some of his devotees were charged with following a deviant sect and apostasy.

Then there was the strange case of Khalil Afandi Abd Hamid and Muhdalena Ahmad, who ran amok outside the Prime Minister's Department on July 9, 2012. The pair had actually just met a week earlier online, where Khalil was posing as a mystic and Muhdalena, a mother of three, decided to follow him on his mad caper.

They arrived at the PM's Department with a samurai sword and took an auxiliary policeman hostage. They then proceeded to smash the windows of cars in the parking area of the complex before an anti-crime squad arrived. Khalil was shot and died from his wounds, while Muhdalena, who was injured, was later acquitted on grounds of insanity.

In yet another cult-like environment, Malaysian-born Siti Aishah Abdul Wahab, who went to the UK as a student in 1967, came under the spell of a rogue communist group led by Singaporean Aravindan Balakrishnan, known as 'Comrade Bala'. In January 2017, he was jailed for 23 years after being found guilty of raping two of his followers and keeping his own daughter Katy as a slave.

His followers were brainwashed into believing in the existence of an invisible machine, dubbed 'Jackie', that he could control using his thoughts. It was their fear of 'Jackie' that allowed Balakrishnan to keep three women as his slaves for 30 years until they were freed in November 2013.

Speaking in 2012 on the Al-Ma'unah incident, the late Karpal Singh recalled: "I defended the leader Amin. I came under fire for defending him but to me it was a point of law. As with the Lim Woon Chong case in the 1970s, I submitted that the 1975 Essential Security Cases (Amendment) Regulations (Escar) was invalid, this time on two grounds.

"Firstly, it gives a right of appeal only to the Supreme Court, which no longer existed, and secondly, the regulations were enacted under an Act passed by reason of the proclamation of emergency in 1969 and that proclamation itself is invalid.

"The whole affair was very strange. If they got that far, why did they stop and wait for the army to come after them? In the meantime, they planned an attack on the breweries and a temple in Batu Caves. What was that about?

"I wanted to get through to Amin and find out what he thought he was doing, but I couldn't penetrate his paranoid mindset. My opinion is that it was part of a failed coup attempt. They did their part and were waiting for more action, and somebody got cold feet."

VERDICT The Al-Ma'unah leaders were executed and their movement crushed, but it is likely that there was more to the incident than will ever be revealed.

25

THE PRINCESS IN THE RAVINE

Date : October 6, 2002
Crime : A model who marries into royalty is dragged from
her car and thrown to her death

Details: In late 2002, small-time actress/model/karaoke hostess, Hasleza Ishak, was found dead from a broken neck in a ravine in Ipoh. It was a case that might not have attracted much attention except for the fact that Hasleza

Actress, model &
karaoke hostess,
Hasleza Ishak.

was said to be the second wife of an important royal figure, the Raja DiHilir of Perak Raja Jaafar Raja Muda Musa. The investigation into Hasleza's death threatened to become a circus when the royal consort Raja Puan Muda Perak Raja Nor Mahani Raja Shahar Shah was briefly called in for questioning.

The events of the case gradually unfolded. On October 6, 2002, Hasleza was driving her Honda City when she was cut off by a Proton Saga. In it were farmer Mat Saad Mat Isa, carpenter Sabarudin Non and fisherman J Manimaran. Mat Saad got down, smashed the Honda's windscreen and proceeded to assault Hasleza.

In the course of the assault, he delivered a strong blow to her neck. An unconscious Hasleeza was then driven to a bridge in the Selama district of Perak. She was dragged out of the car and thrown over the bridge, falling into the ravine and dying instantly.

Mat Saad, Sabarudin and Manimaran were put on trial for Hasleza's murder. Also in the dock were bomoh Rahim Ismail and palace aide Tengku Aristonsjah Tengku Mohamad Ansary, who was a nephew of Raja Mahani.

The Star's News Editor Chelsea LY Ng was then a court reporter covering the case. "These were two women jealously locked in a tug-of-war for Raja Jaafar's heartstrings. They went to the extent of hiring bomohs to cook up spell after spell for them — Raja Mahani with her *tali hidung kerbau* (a rope used to ring the nostrils of a buffalo to make the animal submissive) to 'tame' her husband and Hasleza with a sachet of love potion to captivate him!

"Hasleza's death was real but the testimony given by some of the witnesses seemed frighteningly surreal. We heard Raja Mahani and her aide spilling scandalous stories about the prince and his women — they told the court about the royal household problems, strange happenings in the bewitched palace, and tales of local merlins 'crossing wands' to control the dark forces.

"Raja Mahani also spoke about her ill health, supposedly caused by *santau* (a type of deadly poison made from human hair) Hasleza had used. She then told of the agony she went through vomiting blood and plastic-like substances, losing hair and sleep and the numerous holy men she had seen to help fight the deadly dark arts. We also heard testimonies about the strange behaviour of Raja Jaafar during nightfall and how the love-reviving rope had brought back the passion he once had for his first wife."

Despite this supernatural atmosphere, a very real and chilling crime had occurred. "Such stories drew people from all walks of life to discuss the case, sidelining the more pertinent but infinitely dry evidence like blood DNA tests and telephone call records which provided crucial links for the judge to piece together the puzzle surrounding Hasleza's death."

In fact, Ng recalled, even the media were affected by the case, seeing suspicious activity everywhere and getting more and more wary of potentially superstitious actions like incense burning. A senior lawyer even admitted to avoiding shaking hands with people attending the trial for fear of being placed under a spell!

Over the course of the trial, the pieces fell into place. Midway through the trial, Mat Saad pleaded guilty to an alternative charge of culpable homicide not amounting to murder and was sentenced to 14 years' jail, while Sabarudin and Manimaran were given 20 years each for manslaughter.

Tengku Aristonsjah and Rahim were also convicted and jailed 20 years each for abetting in the killing. However, in August 2006, they were freed following a successful appeal. At the same time, Sabarudin and Manimaran had their sentences reduced to 14 years each. All those involved have thus been released, while Raja Mahani passed away on October 4, 2017.

VERDICT As with some other notorious cases, it appears as if the henchmen served time behind bars, but the mastermind escaped justice.

26

THE CAR PARK ABDUCTION

Date : June 13, 2003
Crime : A newlywed returns to Malaysia for a holiday and
is kidnapped, raped and murdered

Details: IT analyst Canny Ong Lay Kian, 28, had her whole
life ahead of her. Young, beautiful and successful, she was
based in San Diego, California, at the very heart of Silicon
Valley. Canny returned to Malaysia to visit her father, who
was undergoing surgery in Ipoh, and that was when tragedy
struck.

On the eve of her return to the US, Canny attended
a farewell dinner with her mother, sisters and a group of
friends. She went to collect her car from the underground
parking lot and was abducted. After a widely publicised
search, Canny's charred body was found in a manhole near
a highway construction site along Jalan Klang Lama.

When details of her ordeal emerged, it set off a string of
vicious speculation, much of which must have compounded
the agony of Canny's grieving relatives. There were attempts

IT analyst,
Canny Ong.

to link the family to loan sharks and the like. Her mother Pearly Visvanathan bore all rumours bravely, particularly as she had already lost two children earlier, a boy to fever and a baby girl who had drowned.

Michael Chong recalled: "Canny's mother came to see me when her daughter was missing. The more she told me, the more worried I became. I began to prepare for the worst. We were going to begin a broader campaign but the next day they found her body. I felt sorry for the family to be under such stress, but I remember the way it was described to me, the whole case seemed very mysterious."

Indeed, even without lending any credence to such gossip, there can be little doubt that the events that led to Canny Ong's death were simply baffling. It appeared that following dinner at Monte's Restaurant in Bangsar Shopping Complex, Canny had gone to the basement to retrieve the car. It was at this point that she was abducted by aircraft cleaning supervisor Ahmad Najib Aris. He forced her at knife-point to ram the barrier with her mother's

Ahmad Najib at the murder scene. *The Star* file image (courtesy of Star Media Group).

Proton Tiara. Despite this incident, no warning was raised until it was too late.

In the meantime, Canny and Ahmad Najib drove off. Bizarrely, they were spotted at a poorly-lit road shoulder in Kelana Jaya ... by a policeman! Lance Corporal S Ravichandran was suspicious and ordered them to get out of the car on three occasions. However, despite opening her door briefly and seeming to be under duress, Canny did not get down. Ravichandran took their identity cards for inspection but at this point, Ahmad Najib, who was behind the wheel, sped off hastily. Ravichandran fired two shots at the car's front right tyre but failed to stop them.

This, too, was not enough to spark a large manhunt that could have saved Canny's life. The situation became even more tragi-farcical when they had to stop the car because of the tyre. Near the Leisure Commerce Square in Sungai Way, Ahmad Najib got out to attend to the tyre, borrowing a car jack to do so. At this point, onlookers realised that Canny looked to be in some fear. Even though one or two of them actually asked her to get down while he was busy, she refused to leave the car!

Eventually, the opportunity was lost and Ahmad Najib sped off with Canny still under his control. On June 18, her charred body with hands bound was discovered, the Proton Tiara found 3km away.

Within three days, Ahmad Najib was arrested and the evidence was damning. The discovery of Canny's bloodstains on trousers found in his house and a DNA test confirming that he had had intercourse with her just prior to her death made it clear that he was the guilty party. In February 2005, he was sentenced to death for murder and a further 20 years' jail for raping Canny Ong.

Andrew Sagayam covered the case from the very start. "This was a very frustrating case from the very beginning. I think Canny had so many chances to escape. She was a black belt in taekwando, and yet she didn't seem to have made an attempt to break free."

Sagayam remembers going to the security room at Bangsar Shopping Centre right after the abduction. "Another reporter and I saw the footage very briefly. The car banged the barrier and drove off very fast. It looked to us at the time as if there were two other men in the backseat. But we were not allowed to view the footage for long before we were asked to leave. And by the time it came to trial the footage looked as if Ahmad Najib was acting alone.

"Then when they were stopped by the policeman, why didn't she say anything? Could be that he told her he had some people ready to kill her family members if she tried to resist? Maybe he had drugged her. And even after that when they had the flat tyre, people asked him about her and he said she was drunk.

"It was terrible when you think how fate worked against her. In the end, she was raped and then killed brutally. He had to break her knees to fit her into the manhole, then poured kerosene on her and burnt her. Again there are claims that they found sets of footprints near the crime scene, but he was definitely the main player. What his motives were, who knows?"

For all the conspiracy theories, Ahmad Najib appears to have acted alone. A former deputy public prosecutor met him in prison when he was trying to get legal aid for a defamation case.

"He wanted to sue a newspaper agency for saying that he had committed many rapes, but he said he had only committed one. He just looked scary. I saw him and thought this man looked so familiar. When I realised who it was, a chill ran down my spine."

Ahmad Najib was finally hanged on September 23, 2016.

VERDICT Ahmad Najib was found guilty of Canny's murder and sentenced to death.

27

THE MYSTERY OF
THE DROWNED TEEN

Date : September 26, 2004
Crime : A teenage boy is found dead in the swimming pool
of a prominent businessman's house

Details: On the face of it, Chinese teenager Xu Jian Huang
had a good life. He and his older brother, Jian Fei, had
moved to Malaysia to live with a rich relative Koh Kim
Teck and were attending an international school (Mutiara
International Grammar School). But, apparently, behind
the walls of Koh's bungalow in Ampang, the two brothers
were victims of abuse.

The situation reached a tragic conclusion on September
26, 2004, when Jian Huang was found dead in the swimming
pool of the bungalow. Aged just 14, the boy was revealed
in the autopsy to have suffered serious assault before his
death. During the trial, photographs were found on a
handphone of one of Koh's employees showing Jian Huang

Chinese teenager, Xu Jian Huang.

in a squatting position with his hands and legs bound with string. The boy had a terrified expression on his face, and the photograph was believed to have been taken just hours before his death.

So imagine the public outcry when Koh, who was a 'Tan Sri', and his employees Resty Agpalo and Mohamad Najib Zulkifli were acquitted of murdering Jian Huang by the High Court on September 20, 2005. Despite 39 witnesses being called to testify in the case, Justice Abdul Kadir Musa acquitted all three, ruling that the Prosecution had failed to clear many unresolved and unanswered doubts and provide any circumstantial evidence that the three accused had a common intention to murder Jian Huang.

The boy's parents, Xu Jian Lai and Foong Qun Ying, flew in from Europe and China respectively in an attempt to find justice for their son, but none was forthcoming. Despite the incriminating photographs, testimony from the boys' tutor that they were being abused and the findings of the autopsy, there were just too many holes in the Prosecution's case. To compound matters, in 2008, the chairman of a non-profit organisation was detained for allegedly soliciting a RM1 million bribe to 'settle' this case.

Andrew Sagayam, who covered the case, was not satisfied with the outcome. "The boy was murdered because he knew something. When I spoke to the neighbours, they said he was being abused. One story is that he found out something untoward that was going on between some of the occupants in the house and he tried to use that information to stop the abuse.

"Instead, he was killed for it. As a reporter covering the case, I can tell you that there was a lot of secrecy and misinformation surrounding it. Now all those involved have fled the country and I don't think we are ever going to see justice served.

"In fact, all this happened at a time when many high profile cases were going unsolved. There was the murder of Sabah assistant minister of Rural and Entrepreneurial Development Norjan Khan Bahadar (February 11, 2004) and also the case of marketing executive Noritta Samsudin (December 5, 2003). Sadly, none of these cases reached a proper resolution."

Community Policing Malaysia (COPs) founder Kuan Chee Heng said that Jian Huang's death is a sad case of 'enforcers' going too far. "It was overdone. The killers were supposed to intimidate him and rough him up, which itself is wrong. Then they went too far and he died. Another sad part is that the killers got away with it. Probably this should have been charged under culpable homicide, not murder."

Michael Chong is another who was not happy with the case, although his experience was somewhat different. "The case was brought up and it was very big. I was told that the boy's family wanted to come and see me. Somehow it went to the Complaints Bureau in Klang. A man there called Pilot Tan was in charge and he took over. This Pilot Tan made a big hoo-ha saying justice must be served, and he got publicity trying to chase Koh.

"When Koh claimed to be sick in China, Pilot Tan sent people to China. The funny thing is that Pilot Tan himself disappeared and the police were looking for him. It is said that while handling the case he came across some information and he was trying to gain from it financially!"

VERDICT It appears as if Jian Huang's killers have, quite literally, got away with murder. Neither in life nor in death was there enough of an effort made to protect him.

THE CONMAN EXTRAORDINAIRE

Date : January 10, 2006
Crime : A Lebanese immigrant pledges to donate a billion
dollars to charity only to be revealed as a charlatan

Details: At first glance, it seemed to be a generous gesture: an eccentric Arab billionaire announces his commitment to the cause of fighting cancer and backs it up by pledging a mammoth donation of US$275 million (about RM1.02 billion) to the National Cancer Council (Makna) in early 2006.

Elie Youssef Najem, then in his late 40s, said he was a member of an extraordinarily wealthy family, and his pledges were taken at face value by Makna President Mohd Farid Ariffin. It took just a couple of days before Elie's stories began to unravel.

Reports emerged of him being wanted by the police in his native country as well as in Canada. Furthermore, at least five police reports had been filed against him in Malaysia for alleged offences such as criminal breach of trust and

Elie Youssef Najem told many tall tales. *The Star* file image (courtesy of Star Media Group).

non-payment of staff salaries. Surely such a wealthy man couldn't be in such trouble?

Andrew Sagayam was one of the reporters put on Elie's trail and visited him at a luxury condo. "He gained respect by making that huge pledge to Makna. He was a good talker who basically wanted to show off. When I visited him he was talking about how much he loved Malaysia and wanted to contribute to its development, but for all his talking he was quite evasive on where the money was.

"He probably had a bit of money but nowhere near what he claimed. What he did have was a bit of authority. When I visited him he was surrounded by an entourage, and he was snapping his fingers like a sheikh, issuing orders impressively. He was also full of extravagant claims, but if you listened carefully some of them contradicted each other. He said he was royalty, then a self-made tycoon. He said he could walk into Malaysia's Parliament anytime because of his influence and past investment in the country.

In the end, of course, we realised that he was not just a con artist but a little bit off his rocker!"

Michael Chong doesn't mince his words concerning Elie. "This fellow is the biggest conman I have ever seen. When this happened I was very concerned for my friend whose son had cancer. I was thinking that people might believe this Elie if there is a former deputy health minister sitting next to him.

"As soon as he made the announcement so many people came to see me. They said he didn't pay for his furniture. His staff said they weren't paid their salary for many months. The best part is even an Ah Long came to complain to me saying that Elie owed him RM175,000!

"At this time, I heard he was angry with me. I challenged him to sue me, but he never dared. There was one time we saw each other in Berjaya Times Square and he ran away. If today he dares sue me for something, tomorrow I will bring out all the victims."

Less than a week after the donation pledge was announced, Elie was called up for questioning by the police. His marriage to Malaysian teenager Farinnie Farid was also investigated by religious authorities. Pretty soon it was obvious that no one really believed him, yet Elie continued to be in the spotlight, for reasons both farcical and tragic.

In 2007, he claimed he was unjustly left out of *Forbes* magazine's list of the world's richest men! Yet despite his assertions that he owned a bank, he was still unable to pay some of his bills. Eventually, Farinnie tired of their life

Some of the fake notes Elie tried to pass out. *The Star* file image (courtesy of Star Media Group).

together and, during their divorce proceedings, accused him of being abusive.

He soon took up with another partner, Filipina Rosalia Viray. In July 2009, less than three months after they started their relationship, she was found dead, having plunged 14 floors from the De Tropicana condominium in Kuchai Lama where they lived. She was stark naked. The case was judged a suicide.

The next round of trouble came in early 2010 when Elie moved into a 4-star hotel in Bukit Bintang and began giving some extraordinary tips to the staff there. When one of them was unable to change her note at a money changer, the police were called in. They raided his room and discovered a leather bag containing a wad of obviously false US currency … 60 US$1 million bills, 60 US$100,000 bills and 40 US$500 bills which added up to US$66.2 million!

Soon after that, in March 2010, he came up with his latest stunt, announcing plans to produce an autobiographical movie, *The Story of Billionaire Dr Elie Najem*, budgeted at US$88 million (RM288 million). He said he expected 20,000 Malaysians to audition for the movie.

Chong is still amazed that the Elie con went so far. "I still don't know why Malaysians can so easily believe it. Maybe he is clever at remembering important details. He can name all the bank officers and the governors. And he can do it convincingly so that many people believe it's true. And he knows that he can make big claims about a bank but they cannot reveal the details to the press because it is confidential. So in this way he is cunning."

Eventually in August 2010, Elie was sentenced to a total of six years and five months in jail for two counts of cheating and one count of abusing his social visit pass.

In January 2012, when Tanjung Malim-born Kamal Ashnawi declared himself to be a trillionaire and the lawful Emperor of Indonesia, it immediately called to mind Elie Najem and his various follies. Then in 2013, Noor Jan Tuah declared himself to be Sultan of Melaka, although he soon found himself facing charges of cheating four individuals through impersonation, for which he was eventually acquitted. As for Elie, he was last heard writing letters to a reporter, proclaiming his innocence of charges made against him. He is believed to have left the country after serving out his sentence.

VERDICT Elie Youssef Najem is obviously a troubled man, but one with a little bit of charisma. One hopes that since his delusional charades have been exposed, no one will be fooled again.

29

THE MYSTERY OF THE MONGOLIAN MODEL

Date : October 19, 2006
Crime : A missing beauty is found, her body blown up
by dynamite

Details: The story of Altantuya Shaariibuu is arguably one
of the most notorious in Malaysia's history. A beautiful
and mysterious woman, whose past may have included
two divorces and stints as a teacher, model and translator,
Altantuya was alleged to have played a role in negotiations
involving the Malaysian government and foreign companies
over submarine purchases.

What is certain is that she came to Malaysia apparently
in search of commission from those negotiations. She was
reported missing on October 19 by her second cousin
Namiraa Gerelmaa. On November 7, her remains were
found in a deserted forest area in Puncak Alam, Shah Alam,
destroyed by C-4 explosives. What made the case more

Mongolian model,
Altantuya Shaariibuu.

sensational was that Abdul Razak Baginda, who headed the Malaysian Strategic Research Centre think-tank, was charged with abetting her murder.

Razak Baginda was not the only person arrested in connection with Altantuya's murder. Three members of the police force were detained during the murder investigation and the two murder suspects were Chief Inspector Azilah Hadri and Corporal Sirul Azhar Umar, members of the elite Unit Tindakan Khas (the Malaysian Police Special Action Force). Azilah and Sirul were eventually charged with murdering Altantuya on Lot 12843 and Lot 16735 in Mukim Bukit Raja, Selangor, between 10pm on October 19 and 1am on October 20. Investigations by the Malaysian police revealed that she was shot twice before C-4 explosives were used on her body, although it is not certain whether it was the bullets or the explosives that killed her.

The burnt corpse of Altantuya was found at this location. *The Star* file image (courtesy of Star Media Group).

During the trial, numerous distractions occurred. It was alleged that Altantuya had worked with Razak Baginda helping to negotiate the submarine purchases. She was reported to have shown up outside his residence shouting loudly in order to make a scene to embarrass him. She claimed to be pregnant and wanted money to go away. Accusations of impropriety over kickbacks were thrown around.

Sirul's own statement, which he later recanted saying it was made under duress, spoke of a desperate Altantuya, who was whisked away to a remote location and, when realising that her life was in danger, had allegedly begged for her life, citing the unborn child in her belly. But to no avail.

In other controversial testimony, Altantuya's cousin Burmaa Oyunchimeg claimed to have been shown a photograph by Altantuya, allegedly of Altantuya herself, Razak Baginda and then Defence Minister Najib Abdul Razak. Further controversy followed when Karpal Singh, acting on behalf of Altantuya's family, attempted to get said politician to testify at the trial.

While the trial was ongoing, writer/blogger Raja Petra Kamarudin was charged on May 6, 2008, with sedition for linking the politician to the killing. In a sensational statutory declaration on June 18, 2008, Raja Petra then went on to state his belief that the politician's wife was involved in the killing. On July 17, 2008, Raja Petra was charged with three counts of criminal intimidation over that declaration. He eventually fled the country and in April 2011 started giving interviews in which he distanced himself from his own previous allegations.

Yet another contentious issue was the testimony of private investigator P Balasubramaniam. Initially hired by Razak Baginda and part of the Prosecution, he then made two controversial statutory declarations. On July 1, 2008, he made a declaration containing some claims linking certain powerful figures to Altantuya, but a day later, he made a second declaration which did not contain these allegations. Following this retraction, Balasubramaniam went AWOL and appeared to have fled the country, with associates claiming he was in fear for his life and that his family had been threatened.

Eddie Chua covered the case, but found himself as confused as the public. "I flew to Mongolia to follow up there. There were so many loose threads. So many people claiming different things. Some said she was married once, twice. Others said she was never a model. Some said she was still alive in France. You don't know what is true and what is not. Her father took up the case very aggressively and tried to get justice for her but the whole thing still seemed very messy."

Eventually, on October 31, 2008, the High Court acquitted Abdul Razak Baginda of abetment in the murder of Altantuya. Azilah and Sirul, however, were ordered to enter their defence. On April 9, 2009, both former policemen were sentenced to death for the murder of Altantuya, wrapping up the 159-day trial.

Dissatisfied with the verdict, Altantuya's father Dr Shariibuu Setev said he would still proceed with the claim against Razak Baginda, Azilah, Sirul and the Government of Malaysia for damages over his daughter's death.

In February 2013, Balasubramaniam returned from exile, articulating his intention to make a third statutory declaration concerning the case. He also stated that he had testimony that would help bring down the ruling government in the then upcoming May 5 General Election. However, within three weeks of the statement, he was dead from a heart attack. Followers of the case were immediately suspicious, speculating that the dead man had been silenced to prevent any further disclosures.

Later that year, Azilah and Sirul were acquitted of the murder by the Court of Appeal. In its findings on August 23, 2013, the panel chaired by future attorney-general Apandi Ali ruled that the trial judge had erred by not examining whether the contradictions and inconsistencies in the Prosecution witnesses' testimony was material. They also said that further finding should have been made connecting the explosives to the accused.

Things took yet another turn on January 13, 2015, when the Federal Court overturned the appeal verdict and upheld the original sentence. The judges ruled that the Prosecution had indeed proved its case beyond a reasonable doubt. What was strange is that while Azilah was at the hearing, Sirul was nowhere to be seen. He had in fact fled the country!

Sirul had fled to Australia where he was detained by immigration after Interpol issued a high priority notice on him. He has been staying in a detention centre there since 2015, and has sought asylum, claiming he would be hanged if he returned to Malaysia. According to a media source in Australia, politicians from both sides of Malaysia's political divide sought contact with Sirul.

A highly-placed source said: "I am sorry to say this but it is my belief that Altantuya herself was playing a dangerous game, and she was trying to be too clever. She had some information with which she was trying to blackmail some quite high-ranking officials. However, it did not go all the way up to Najib. Whether it was personal or financial I am not certain, but she paid for it with her life."

Kuan Chee Heng is adamant that the case was twisted for political purposes. "From my sources, I can tell you — I put my head on the block and say that Najib and his wife Rosmah Mansor were not involved in any way. In this case, they are innocent and political opponents have linked them unfairly.

"This was another case where the killers went too far. They received instructions to deal with Altantuya, which were meant to intimidate her into leaving the country and not returning. Send her to Mongolia or Timbuktu, not to kill her. These guys misunderstood and killed her instead."

Following the Pakatan Harapan victory in the general election of May 9, 2018, the newly elected Prime Minister Dr Mahathir Mohamad discussed the possibility of commuting Sirul's death sentence to allow him to testify in a reopened case. Sirul is demanding full immunity before returning.

On June 20, 2018, Dr Setev met with Mahathir and his lawyer Ramkarpal Singh, then informed the press that new Attorney General Tommy Thomas was amenable to re-opening the case.

Further drama ensued in December 2019 when Azilah made a series of explosive allegations in a statutory declaration. He sensationally accused Najib Abdul Razak and Razak Baginda of ordering the killing of the Mongolian national. He said that they had both told him that Altantuya was a foreign spy, who was a threat to national security.

Najib, in turn, dismissed the accusations as lies told by a desperate man trying to escape a death sentence.

VERDICT The two former policemen have been sentenced to death, but questions remain over their motives, and if they were the sole parties responsible.

30

TORTURE HORROR

Date : August 20, 2007
Crime : An eight-year-old girl is abducted and cruelly
murdered

Details: Nurin Jazlin Jazimin was a beautiful little girl who went missing on August 20, 2007, just before her eighth birthday. She had gone to a *pasar malam* (night market) near her house in Wangsa Maju, Kuala Lumpur to buy a hairclip. After the revelation that she had been seen dragged into a white van, a nationwide hunt was launched for the missing Nurin.

Tragically, on the morning of September 17, 2007, just six days after Nurin turned eight, her body was found in a gym bag in front of a shop lot in PJS 1/48, Petaling Jaya, Selangor. Her body was almost unrecognisable and she had been sexually assaulted. Her grief-stricken parents were barely able to recognise her but DNA tests later confirmed that the body was indeed that of Nurin.

Andrew Sagayam covered the Nurin case and remembers

Nurin Jazlin Jazimin went missing on August 20, 2007.

it as being one of the most heart-breaking crimes he's seen. "As a crime reporter, you have to harden your heart and not get too personally involved otherwise you won't be able to do your job. Sometimes you see things that will make you give up on humans. What happened with Nurin was like that. She was tortured sexually and then killed.

"I think the main line of enquiry in this case was looking at the possibility of kidnap for child pornography purposes. At that time, there were many cases of cute young children who were abducted and never seen again. I remember it was published that Nurin was one of 17 children under the age of nine on the police's list of missing persons, who were taken between January and August 2007. There were other stories that floated, some said there was a grudge against the family, and others talked about a Kampung Baru molester, but I believe it was the child pornography angle that is the real motive in this case."

Nurin's parents suffered further trauma and judgement when a senior police official suggested that the police might investigate whether her disappearance was due to their negligence. Despite what seemed like a strong lead when a man on a motorcycle was pictured on CCTV dumping the gym bag, all follow-ups on the Nurin case led to dead ends. On September 28, 2007, four men and a woman were arrested in connection with the murder but they were all released unconditionally within three days.

Michael Chong recalled the case with sadness. "When this thing happened, I was expecting the family to come to me, but they never did. I took this case out of pity. I personally offered a reward of RM20,000 for any information that could save her. We printed out pamphlets and went around the area.

"The funny thing is there was nothing. No one took up the offer. Not even one prank call. Normally we have drug addicts or some jokers who want to get the money but in this case there was nothing. We tried our best, everyone working together but there was no luck. In fact, after Nurin's case, there were so many.

"In one case, we managed to track down a boy who was kidnapped. He was a hyperactive child and he was kept by some Indonesians in an illegal house. I think they had some dispute and some of them tried to claim the reward, but I think the police were suspicious and they were detained instead."

Another high-powered source had some chilling testimony. "We think there aren't psychologically sick people in our society, but there must be. There must even be serial killers who prey on children. And how do they get away with it? The criminal is most likely in a position to hide his tracks. Maybe he is a powerful politician or extremely wealthy individual. They might be in cahoots with a rogue policeman to help to cover up such crimes."

Tragically, despite reward offers and the involvement of the police, NGOs and government ministries, Nurin's killer has never been found.

VERDICT What happened to Nurin is every parent's nightmare. Her sadistic killer is still on the loose.

31

DEATH IN CUSTODY

Date : January 20, 2009
Crime : A young man is found beaten to death in police custody, highlighting a silent epidemic

Details: An able-bodied young man, A Kugan was detained for questioning by police for suspected car theft. After a five-day spell in the lock-up, Kugan, 23, was found dead. A rushed autopsy indicated he had died due to fluid accumulation in the lungs, but an angry crowd led by Kugan's family and several politicians stormed the morgue at Serdang Hospital. In examining his body, they found clear signs of torture. A second autopsy was ordered revealing that Kugan had been beaten, burned and starved prior to his death, and the case was later re-classified as murder.

Andrew Sagayam said: "The word on the ground is that Kugan was linked to a car-theft gang. He was also a bit cocky and at one point spilled some information that interfered

Police detainee,
A Kugan.

with a police raid. Another story is that someone inside the police station was linked to a rival car gang. Whatever the reason, Kugan was tortured inside the station and it got out of hand, killing him."

After public outcry, a few police officers were transferred out, but only one, V Navindran, was charged with two counts of causing grievous hurt to Kugan while the latter was in custody. However, on January 28, 2011, Navindran was acquitted after the judge found him not guilty citing that the Prosecution had failed to establish a *prima facie* case against him.

While Kugan's case may now have been forgotten, it begs the question why people die in police custody, which theoretically should be one of the safest places for any country's citizens. This may seem like a simple question, but examining just why so many lives have been extinguished in police stations and prisons raises issues that society seems disinclined to confront.

Deaths in custody can occur as a result of suicide, murder by other detainees or genuine ill health. What's perturbing is the possibility that some deaths could result from torture and abuse on the part of the authorities themselves. Yet, not once in Malaysia has this resulted in a conviction for murder. Does this mean that those in authority can kill with impunity?

"This is a real issue," said Simon Sipaun, who served on the human rights board Suhakam for over 10 years from 2000–2010. "The mother of all rights is the right to life. Suhakam has a standing decision that since the law (section 334 of the Criminal Procedure Code) requires an inquest in the event of custodial death, we will undertake a public inquiry if no inquest is conducted. Often, when the authorities receive such a notification from us, they hastily commence the inquest!"

Sipaun is dissatisfied with the results these inquests produce. "I don't remember any prosecution emerging from these investigations. For a start, in the case of suspicious deaths, you have to make a report to the police, and chances are they will defend their own kind.

"The police are very defensive and people get the impression that the fault is with police. Many times during my visits to lock-ups after a suspicious death, the official explanations do not tally. You'd think it should be easy enough to find evidence indicating the cause of death, but often, crucial evidence is not forthcoming. For example, if there is supposed to be a camera at the police station where a death had occurred, it would either be missing or not working."

His views are supported by lawyer N Surendran, who was involved in the case of Francis Udayappan, whose disappearance and death after his detention at the Brickfields police station in Kuala Lumpur on April 16, 2004, highlighted the many flaws in operating procedures.

Udayappan, 24, reportedly escaped from custody and initially, there was conflicting evidence as to whether a partially decomposed body found in the nearby Klang River was his.

Surendran also served as counsel in Kugan's case and he clearly still feels passionately about the issue. "To me, most deaths in custody are suspicious. Even if a person is genuinely sick and then dies, doesn't that raise the question of negligence?

"But in my years of covering cases of police brutality and deaths in custody, I have seen almost no action taken against the offenders. The only one that stands out is the case of B Prabakar, who was beaten with a rubber hose and scalded with hot water in December 2008."

The treatment meted out to car park attendant Prabakar, 28, resulted in seven Crime Investigation Department (CID) officers being charged with voluntarily causing hurt. "In that case, we had photographic evidence and the pictures were widely distributed." But in most other cases, he said, things can be covered up, thus no action is taken.

Surendran has personally witnessed torture in police

stations. "In October 2005, I was with S Manickavasagam (later an MP for Kapar) visiting the Banting District police headquarters on another matter, when we saw a man being tortured in an interrogation room. His arms were twisted behind his back and he was gagged. He was crying, but the policemen torturing him were laughing. We reported the matter, but until today no action has been taken."

Activist Nathaniel Tan was sufficiently angered by the injustice of such deaths that he authored *Where is Justice? Death and Brutality in Custody*, a book which highlights some of the many flaws in our system. As if to prove there was more political will involved in suppressing rather than exposing such perceived injustice, copies of the book were confiscated by the police and the Home Ministry, although it was not banned.

Former Inspector-General of Police Hanif Omar has come out firmly against the abuse of power that can lead to deaths in custody. In his column, 'Point of View' in *The Star* on April 9, 2006 ('Stand firmly behind wheel of reform'), he wrote that "it would be foolhardy for the police to allow any uncalled-for deaths to occur on their watch".

He also suggested having special magistrates investigate suspicious deaths in custody. "This is because our normal magistrates are trained in the adversarial format whereas I believe that an inquiring magistrate may have to play an inquisitorial role."

Surendran said: "We cannot expect any positive developments until an independent mechanism has been put into place. At present, victims have to go back to the police, who are not likely to impartially investigate a crime that could implicate fellow officers.

"In cases when some action is taken to appease public anger, the officers are likely to be charged with lesser offences even when it is a clear case of murder. Most cases don't get solved and the police have nothing to fear. Custodial deaths happen everywhere, but in countries that have an independent body to investigate such deaths, there is at least some accountability."

An interview with a junior police officer proved telling. "The higher-ups won't talk" he said. "And I don't blame them. This issue is being blown out of proportion. It is very easy for the public to make police seem like we are trigger-happy as in the case of Aminulrasyid Amzah (a 15-year-old who was shot dead in Shah Alam, Selangor on April 26, 2010, after being chased by police officers). They think we are bad guys who beat up innocent people, but they don't know what we are dealing with. Most police officers put their lives on the line for very little pay and we encounter dangerous criminals on a daily basis.

"Many of the criminals are arrogant and provocative. Sometimes the criminal is withholding crucial information which could help save the life of an innocent person, even a small child. At times like that, the interrogation can get out of hand. There are a few bad hats in the police force, but they are a small minority. As far as I know, I have never seen a police officer beat someone who was innocent!"

Shockingly, this same police officer we interviewed was later implicated in another lock-up death, that of N

Dharmendran who died in custody on May 21, 2013. Dharmendran suffered 52 injuries and even had a stapled ear. This officer was one of four policemen tried, acquitted and discharged in connection with Dharmendran's death.

Forensic psychiatrist Dr Muhammad Muhsin Ahmad Zahari explained the standard medical procedure in the event of a suspicious death. "When there is an unnatural death or suspected foul play, the burial certificate cannot be produced immediately. There is a need to conduct a postmortem to determine the cause of death," he said. Identifying the medical evidence would satisfy interested parties such as the police, prison authorities and family members.

"The possibility of suicide is very important," Dr Muhsin added. "Physical evidence of hanging or an overdose or other possible methods of suicide could be a crucial finding for death in detention." There is also the need to address death from illnesses, such as asthma, epilepsy, diabetes, stroke or heart attack.

"Death from medical illness is far higher than other causes of death in detention. From 1999 to 2008, for example, there were 2,571 deaths among prisoners suffering from medical illnesses, particularly HIV and TB. This means that the health service in the custodial setting has to be improved. It is important to have a system to deal with medical emergencies. The only people who should be authorised to carry out treatment are medical personnel. Hence, if there is any hint of a serious illness, police officers and custodial officers have to refer to the standard healthcare system. Failure to do this amounts to negligence."

Michael Chong also feels that those who go into the lock-up may need special protection. "Lock-up cases are tricky. I have never ever had a brutality case, but many times the family will call me saying their loved one is in the lock-up and they are worried about them. I will give a friendly call to make sure they are given proper treatment and access to medical care if needed. In all my cases, not one of them has been touched."

A racial element to these deaths is also undeniable. A disproportionately large percentage of the deaths in custody involve those of Indian ethnicity. According to figures by human rights group Suaram, there were 257 deaths in police custody between 2002 and 2016. Of these, 42.4% were Malays, 23.4% Indians, 18.3% Chinese, 12.8% foreign nationals and 3.1% other Malaysian minorities.

But reports carried by *The Star* over a 15-year period from 1996 to 2011 show that nearly 80% of custodial deaths reported involved Indians! Is there some discrepancy somewhere? Is the issue merely underreporting of deaths by the Malay community or falsifying of data by the police?

Could the same people who think nothing of torturing detainees also be responsible for fudging the statistics?

Given that Indians make up only about 7% of the population, either number is disproportionately high. According to Amnesty International research on police brutality and custodial deaths, this mirrors the trends of victimisation of African-American males in the USA, male

Aborigines in Australia and males of African descent in France.

Sipaun said: "I noticed that more often than not, when Suhakam received a complaint about a suspicious death, it involved those of Indian ethnicity. Even during my time on Suhakam's Complaints and Inquiries Working Group, I noted that most of those arrested under the Emergency Ordinance were Indians."

After the death of S Balamurugan in custody at the Klang Utara police headquarters on February 8, 2017, an Enforcement Agency Integrity Commission hearing was held. Witnesses told that the deceased was shivering uncontrollably, asked for help and had an underlying heart condition. When his wife went to visit him, she was not able to see him but could hear him screaming for help. He was sent to the Klang Magistrate's Court where he vomited blood, but the court refused a police request for a remand order instructing that he be taken to hospital immediately. Instead, he was taken back to lock-up and died there shortly after. Everything about it reeks of injustice.

Social activist Janakey Raman of the Nationwide Human Development and Research Centre has spent most of his life working with estate communities. He said the fear among the Indian community is that they have been targeted and branded as criminals.

"On the ground, people don't know what the truth is. In the Tamil press, the issue of lock-up deaths is covered very emotionally, and people don't know what to believe. Are those who die in lock-ups gangsters or innocents? Either way, so many young healthy men shouldn't be dying in the lock-ups.

"I think it is a socio-economic problem. Youths migrate from estates, they can't find proper jobs and fall into professions, including gangsterism, that expose them to violence and at the same time make them vulnerable. As social workers, we try to train the youths to realise that education is the key to avoiding being caught in this situation."

While the factors that lead to deaths in custody can be debated, what is clear is that the issue is not being addressed properly. As long as there is no political will to improve the lot of a disenfranchised group of society, the next tragedy could just be around the corner. In May 2019, newly appointed Inspector-General of Police Abdul Hamid Bador announced the formation of the Independent Police Complaints and Misconduct Commission (IPCMC), giving some hope that with a monitoring body, this trend might be checked.

VERDICT No one has been convicted of causing Kugan's death and those of many other people, particularly young men of Indian ethnicity, which continues at an alarming rate.

32

A FALLEN COMRADE

Date : July 16, 2009
Crime : A political aide is found dead after going into the
MACC for questioning

Details: While the authors have attempted to deal with most of these cases in a dispassionate manner and with as balanced a viewpoint as possible, the Teoh Beng Hock case is a particularly painful one for Martin Vengadesan to address. Quite simply, Teoh was a personal friend, from the time the duo were sent on the same assignment in Seoul, South Korea, in February 2006.

They spoke often after that trip and Martin recalls encouraging him to make the switch from journalism to politics. The opportunity arose sooner than imagined when following the March 8, 2008 General Election, Teoh quit working for the *Sin Chew Jit Poh* newspaper to work as a political aide to Seri Kembangan assemblyman Ean Yong Hian Wah. Suddenly, it was Teoh who was too busy to catch up. Not for a moment did Martin envisage the tragedy that would befall Teoh.

On July 16, 2009, the day before he was due to register his marriage to teacher Soh Cher Wei, Teoh was found dead on the fifth floor of Plaza Masalam in Shah Alam. He had fallen from the 14th floor of that building which housed the Selangor Malaysian Anti-Corruption Commission (MACC) office.

The official post-mortem found that Teoh died as the result of internal injuries sustained in a fall. But why did he die? Was he pushed? Was it an accident? Was it suicide? Fuelled by grief, Teoh's family and friends led the demand for answers.

Martin took a drive down to his hometown of Melaka to pay his last respects and aside from the shell-shocked feeling that many of us had, there was a firm resolve that whoever had done this to Teoh must be brought to justice.

During the inquest into Teoh's death which began on August 8, 2009, the story emerged of how Teoh had been subjected to an unnecessary strenuous and aggressive round of questioning. The events leading to his death began with a raid on Ean Yong Hian Wah's office in the Selangor State Secretariat building by MACC officers at 4.30pm, July 15, 2009. This was seen as part of the MACC's investigation into graft allegations made against the Selangor Pakatan Rakyat state government.

Following the raid, Teoh was brought to the MACC Selangor headquarters to endure a marathon interrogation, which lasted nine hours from 5pm on July 15. He was denied access to a lawyer and only released at 3.45am on July 16, according to the MACC. He then re-appeared at the MACC headquarters in the morning only to be found dead at 1.30pm.

Critically, during the inquest, famed Thai pathologist Dr Pornthip Rojanasunand testified that in her opinion, there was an 80% chance that Teoh's death was a homicide. However, this was countered by another pathologist who felt that it could not have been a homicide. During the lengthy inquest, a number of mysterious letters and notes surfaced to complicate the issue.

Eventually, on January 5, 2011, the coroner Azmil Mustapha Abas delivered an open verdict, yet ruled out both suicide and homicide as the cause of death. This was such an unpopular decision that the clamour for a Royal Commission of Inquiry (RCI) was heeded.

On July 21, 2011, more than two years after Teoh's death, the RCI published a 124-page report stating that Teoh had been driven to commit suicide by 'aggressive, relentless, oppressive and unscrupulous' interrogation by three MACC officers.

They were named as Selangor MACC Deputy Director Hishamuddin Hashim and his officers Mohamad Anuar Ismail and Ashraf Mohd Yunus. The Commission said that unlawful intimidatory tactics used 'would have had grave consequences upon Beng Hock's mind and would have been a culminating factor that drove him to suicide'.

In a further blow to the MACC's credibility, Selangor Customs assistant director Ahmad Sarbani Mohamed was found dead at the MACC headquarters in Jalan Cochrane on April 6, 2011. Despite similarly suspicious circumstances, on September 26, 2011, coroner Aizatul Akmal Maharani ruled the death accidental and a result of 'misadventure'.

On September 5, 2014, the Court of Appeal set aside the original coroner's open verdict and ruled out that he had committed suicide. The panel said that his death was caused by multiple injuries from a fall that was a result of, or which was accelerated by, an unlawful act or acts of persons unknown, inclusive of MACC officers who were involved in his arrest and investigation. But no one was brought up on the charges.

Following the fall of Umno and the victory of the Pakatan Harapan government on May 9, 2018, it was announced by the Cabinet on June 20, 2018, that they had decided to re-open the probe into Teoh's death and that the Attorney General had been asked to proceed.

However, on June 25, 2019, Teoh Beng Hock Trust for Democracy Chairperson Ng Geok Chee said they learnt that police had reopened their investigation into Teoh's death under section 342 of the Penal Code for wrongful confinement. The group learnt about the reclassification of the investigation after police summoned Teoh's sister, Lee Lan, to facilitate their investigation under section 342.

They have called for his case to be investigated under culpable homicide which carries a stiffer penalty. His family still rejects the possibility of suicide and are convinced that he was murdered. The cries of 'Justice for Beng Hock' will not be silenced.

VERDICT A good man died under pressure from an aggressive interrogation. We await more details.

33

THE BANTING MURDERS

Date : August 30, 2010
Crime : One of Malaysia's richest women goes missing,
leading to the discovery of multiple corpses

Details: Sosilawati Lawiya was truly a Malaysian success story.
She worked her way up from being a clerk to head her own
cosmetics business, one which had over 300 outlets, making
her one of the richest women in the country.

She was briefly married to rock star Nash, the former
lead singer of hard rock band Lefthanded, and had six
children from an earlier marriage.

It all went tragically wrong on August 30, 2010. Firstly,
Sosilawati's eldest daughter Erni Dekriwati received a
mysterious text message from her mother. It warned her not
to let a certain employee into the family home and implied
that compromising photographs of her (Sosilawati) had
been taken. After this she went silent.

Her daughter then tried to reach her repeatedly but to
no avail. After an extensive police hunt, it was revealed that

Successful Malaysian businesswoman, Sosilawati Lawiya.

Sosilawati and three others — lawyer Ahmad Kamil Abdul Karim, bank officer Noorhisham Mohammad and driver Kamaruddin Shamsuddin — were also missing. The quartet were believed to have gone to Banting to discuss a land deal.

Soon after, Sosilawati's BMW was found abandoned and the lawyers they were supposed to have met up with fell under suspicion.

The lawyers were N Pathmanabhan and his brother N Surendran (not the parliamentarian and human rights lawyer).

It was revealed that a meeting had taken place near the lawyers' house before the victims were taken to an oil palm estate in Sungai Gadung.

The four were allegedly beaten up and repeatedly stabbed before they were torched. Their ashes were then allegedly scattered into rivers and streams near the farm and surrounding areas.

A fortnight after their disappearance on September 12, the two lawyer brothers and six others were arrested.

Eventually, Pathmanabhan and three others who worked as helpers on his estate, T Thilaiyalagan, R Matan and R Kathavarayan, were jointly charged in Banting on October 13, 2010.

But what led to the grisly murders?

As the trial evolved, it was revealed that on many previous occasions, those who had business meetings with Pathmanabhan had disappeared and family members of those who went missing had filed police reports.

Most are believed to have had land dealings with Pathmanabhan, leading to the theory that it was his practice to carry out underhanded deals and order the murder of those in a position to expose him.

Among the missing individuals were lawyers R Thinakaran Raman, SP Annamalai, Chew Sien Chee, S Pathmanathan and Triptipal Singh. All the lawyers had been practising in Penang and were believed to have been murdered between 1992 and 2009.

The court also heard the testimony of S Usharani, the widow of missing Indian businessman A Muthuraja, who said that her husband had been lured to Malaysia by the brothers. She told the court that he had tried to extricate himself from dealings with the brothers but had gone missing instead.

Investigations also uncovered the murder of housewife T Selvi, 44, who was attacked outside her house in Banting in December 2008. She had allegedly lent the accused a large sum of money and had pressed for payment which ultimately led to her death.

In a testimony in the High Court, DPP Saiful Edris Zainuddin said that Sosilawati and her group went to Banting on that fateful day to meet Pathmanabhan to discuss land matters and to expedite a RM3 million cheque dated September 9, 2010.

Sosilawati had wanted to use the money to give bonuses to her staff ahead of the Hari Raya festivity that fell on September 10 that year.

Matters came to a head when Pathmanabhan could not come up with RM3 million to pay her, and her group was assaulted and killed.

While searching the estate and the nearby rivers and jungle, the police found human bone fragments and several personal effects belonging to the victims, as well as knives that might have been used in the murders.

However, the one factor that made it hard to prosecute the accused for murder was the absence of any bodies!

In the entire history of Malaysian law, this had only happened once before in 1963, in a case involving budding racing driver Sunny Ang, whose girlfriend went missing during a diving trip, three weeks after she had signed a will handing everything over to his mother.

It is believed that for this reason, the Prosecution had no choice but to go after only some, not all of those involved.

Pathmanabhan's brother, Surendran, was not charged while U Suresh and K Sarawanan became Prosecution witnesses after they pleaded guilty to a lesser charge of disposing of the murder evidence. They were initially given a sentence of seven years in prison each, but are now serving a 20-year term each in the Sungai Udang Prison in Melaka after the Court of Appeal increased their sentence.

Andrew Sagayam said: "One of the issues that kept cropping up with the Sosilawati case is how they were able to get away with it for so long. After all, so many missing persons reports were filed, so how did the investigations not reveal what was going on?

"The only logical conclusion is that this Pathmanabhan, who was a 'Datuk', was in cahoots with cops at the local level. They must have been on the payroll and closing one eye to what was going on. It was probably because of that which led to the brothers becoming more and more bold!

"That's why when such a high-profile victim made the disappearances impossible to ignore, it led to a shake-up in the investigating police force as well."

Andrew also pointed out that staff at the Kuala Langat Land Office were supposed to be questioned in connection with the allegations of fraud involving land transactions with a value of more than RM7 million.

"I sincerely believe that the brothers could have continued to get away with it had they not picked such a public figure like Sosilawati for a target. That's what is terrifying about the lawlessness that existed there."

Eventually, on March 17, 2017, the Federal Court dismissed the appeals and upheld the convictions of Pathmanabhan, Thilaiyalagan and Kathavarayan while sensationally acquitting and discharging Matan due to insufficient evidence.

Chief Justice Arifin Zakaria said that there was

'overwhelming evidence before the court to show that Sosilawati and the three others were murdered at the farm within the time and on the date stated in the charges, and that their murders were committed by the three men acting with common intention'.

"There was violence in this case. Bloodstains of the deceased persons were found on the bat, two zinc sheets and wall of the farm house. Unless there was violence, no blood would have been splattered on the wall," he said, adding that the four bodies were incinerated.

VERDICT Not everyone culpable in the homicides has been punished, particularly those who became Prosecution witnesses and corrupt officials who helped to hide past crimes.

34

THE NAJADI SLAYING

Date : July 29, 2013
Crime : A prominent banker and his wife are shot in broad daylight

Details: On a quiet Monday afternoon, an elderly gentleman and his spouse leave a Buddhist temple. From out of nowhere, an assailant emerges firing shots. The old man is fatally hit and his wife is injured, while the killer flees in a waiting taxi. Why such a mindless crime? Why would a senior citizen be a victim of a deliberate shooting?

When the dust had settled, the identity of the dead man seemed to provide some understanding as to why he was targeted.

He was Hussain Najadi, 75, born in Persia. An Iranian citizen with Malaysian PR status, he had established AmBank in 1975, and was chairman and chief executive officer of the AIAK Group at the time of his death. His wife Cheong Mei Kuen, 49, was shot in the left hand and right leg, but survived the shooting.

The police first managed to get a lead by catching hold of the taxi driver involved in the getaway, one Chew Siang Chee. Chew in turn led them to a man he said was the killer, a man known as both Ah Kwan and by his nickname Sei Ngan Chai (four-eyed man). The alleged gunman's real name was Koong Swee Kwan, a tow truck driver.

Surprisingly, given the mystery behind the killing, Koong was tracked down swiftly and charged with Najadi's murder, as well as the attempted murder of Cheong. However, Koong appeared to be just a hired hand. He was revealed to have been paid RM20,000 for Najadi's killing, although no motive was forthcoming. He originally indicated that a triad figure named Lim Yuen Soo was the one who had hired him to carry out the killing, but he did not know why.

On September 5, 2014, the High Court convicted Koong of the offences and sentenced him to death. However, on December 14, 2016, the Federal Court set aside the conviction and ordered the case to be retried in the High Court.

It's worth noting that while investigating this lead, the police had actually arrested Lim in October 2015. However, they released him after just eight days due to a lack of evidence linking him to the case. An Interpol red notice arrest warrant had been issued for Lim in connection with the case and he was apprehended when flying back to Malaysia from China. Yet he was released without any further action being taken.

The taxi driver Chew was originally sentenced on

February 17, 2014, to a total of 14 years' jail and six strokes of the rotan for possessing a Walther pistol, a magazine and four bullets. After serving nearly two years of that sentence, he was freed by the Court of Appeal on February 12, 2016.

Najadi's son from an earlier marriage, Pascal Najadi, who was based first in Russia and then Switzerland, has maintained that his father was the victim of a RM30 million murder contract. While some tried to link the murder to a real estate dispute over valuable land occupied by a temple, Pascal believes that his late father had knowledge of massive financial impropriety.

Pascal stated his belief that his father's death was linked to the great financial scandal of Malaysia, the 1Malaysia Development Berhad (1MDB), where billions of ringgit were allegedly misappropriated. He claimed that his father had voiced concerns about AmBank operations and also said he had refused a lucrative but tainted offer from Umno representatives.

Pascal told whistleblower site *The Sarawak Report* that at their last meeting, his father had complained about massive corruption. "He also said that they (people in power) had lost the plot and recklessly, behind their own population's backs, raked in billions of ringgit from construction, oil & gas to defence and transportation. He made a point that it's insane that they do not for one second think about the future generations."

He argued that there was no discernible effort made by investigators to produce a compelling motive for his father's killing. He said it was accepted that Koong was paid to kill Najadi, but nobody knew why.

Kuan Chee Heng vehemently disagreed. "This was truly mistaken identity. And certainly nothing to do with the 1MDB case. Najadi was not on any hit list at all. The hired killer really mistook him for someone else. Some politicians make it as though it is a plotted murder but actually he got the wrong guy and it was not even supposed to be a murder. The truth is untold."

Kuan, also known as Uncle Kentang for his charity work, believes that the issue had nothing to do with banking whatsoever. The location of the murder, he said, was actually key to the motive.

"What got him there in the first place? It was to protect the Kuan Yin Temple in Jalan Ceylon from a land grab."

The temple was on a parcel of land worth some RM40 million that was being negotiated for sale. Indeed, then city CID Chief Senior Assistant Commissioner Ku Chin Wah told the press that Najadi was not a buyer or a seller involved in the deal but was asked to help protect the temple from any deal.

The problem, Kuan claimed, was that Koong was on drugs and had completely misunderstood his instructions. "There was supposed to be a table talk to negotiate this issue. Somehow Koong got the identity wrong and the instructions wrong. There was supposed to be an Indian 'Datuk' present and Koong mistook Najadi for him."

Andrew Sagayam said: "This was another case with many conspiracy theories. What we can clearly see is that the masterminds behind the murder, whether it's deliberate or mistaken identity, have not been caught. Koong was a hired killer, but the trail went cold, most likely deliberately so."

When the case was retried, Cheong took to the stand, giving an emotional victim impact statement. She said that she had become reclusive and bedridden after the traumatic killing and that she was reduced to reliving the moment over and over again in her mind, saying that others had been able to move on with their lives, but she had not. "I lost a husband who was the salt of the earth. My mental state cannot be restored, and it is beyond comprehension how a person could do this to another human being," she told the court.

Finally, on October 28, 2017, the case culminated. Koong was sentenced to death for Najadi's murder and 18 years for the attempted murder of Cheong. Despite the conviction, Pascal still feels it was part of a cover-up. "With Koong's execution, any information he has will die with him," he said.

VERDICT Koong Swee Kwan has been sentenced to death, but those who ordered Najadi's killing have got away with it.

35

THE COSPLAY KILLER

Date : October 21, 2013
Crime : A teenager agrees to meet an online friend to work on their costumes, but she never makes it back alive

Details: Many subcultures of fantasy, science fiction, graphic novels and comic books exist. There are followers who get into the dimensions of the Batmobile and learn how to wield a lightsaber, gamers who dress as mages, fanboys who speak Klingon and others who are obsessed with *Lord of the Rings.*

The cosplay subculture is shared by lots of people across many different fan groups. It is made up largely of people who have a fondness for dressing up as their favourite characters from books, films, TV series, comic books, music and more. Probably the most famous point of origin of cosplay is Japan, where anime and manga characters are still the most popular.

These cosplay fans usually have conventions and meet online in chat rooms or Facebook groups and the like.

Fifteen-year-old Ng Yuk Tim was one such person. She had just finished her Form 3 exams and was looking to unwind.

One of her online friends was the older Poon Wai Hong, 23, who was also part of the broader cosplay community.

The pair chatted on Facebook and got along well. He then invited the teen to his home suggesting that they work on their costumes together. It was to be the last time anyone saw her alive.

What is clear is that she left her home in Bandar Tun Razak at 11am and took the LRT to the Kelana Jaya station, where she met Poon. He brought her to his house in Kampung Cempaka in Petaling Jaya, a short distance from the Kelana Jaya LRT station.

When questioned later, Poon said that there had been a number of visitors to his house including a lorry driver and someone who had come to rent materials from him. According to him, after their session ended he dropped her off at the Kelana Jaya LRT station at about 3.30pm. She was nowhere to be found after that.

A search was launched for Ng and a distraught Poon was among the most determined to find the missing girl. Kuan Chee Heng was also among those searching for the girl. He noticed something amiss when he started talking to Poon during the search.

"He said nobody saw him and the girl in the house and no neighbours saw them leaving. I got suspicious when I started to question him about when the girl was in his house," said Kuan.

Kuan said his suspicions were aroused because Poon started giving him very vivid and precise details, almost as if he had rehearsed his story.

"He gave me an exact play-by-play right down to what he was holding in his hands at the time," Kuan said.

Kuan also noted that Poon had initially made a show of sending out concerned text messages and making calls to the missing girl but had given up abruptly early Tuesday morning, which also aroused his suspicions.

Finally, in the midst of the search, Kuan questioned Poon again, making it clear that he doubted his story. This time, Poon cracked, telling a different story.

Poon said that Ng had visited him at a time when both were alone in the house. He had become overwhelmed with desire and attempted to engage in sexual contact. When she resisted, he became angry and struck her on the head with a dumbbell he used for exercise.

He maintained that it was wholly an accident but that he had panicked and packed the girl's body in a suitcase. He proceeded to dump the suitcase containing her body along the roadside at Jalan Kebun Nenas, Shah Alam.

Soon after his confession, Poon was asked to lead the police to Ng's body which he did. He was arrested and charged with her murder.

When asked by waiting reporters if he regretted his actions, all he had to say was, "It's too late for me to regret."

Ng's tragic death also shook the cosplay community, where members often build virtual relationships of trust with each other. It brought into focus the dangers of connecting with strangers online and then meeting with them in person at private locations.

Although Poon continued to claim that Ng's death was an accident, the trial judge ordered a mandatory death penalty. On April 3, 2018, he was sentenced to death for her murder.

"This is another sad case all around," said Kuan. "She was young and too trusting. He came from a broken home and there was nothing premeditated about the crime. He tried something which he shouldn't have, she rejected him, he overreacted and now two lives are gone."

VERDICT Poon Wai Hong was sentenced to hang for the murder of an innocent teen.

36

THE MISSING PLANE

Date : March 8, 2014
Crime : Flight MH370 disappears en route to China, spawning
the greatest aviation mystery of our time

Details: Perhaps no single tragedy is as deeply and freshly imprinted on the collective Malaysian consciousness as that of the disappearance of Malaysia Airlines flight MH370. The May 13, 1969 racial riots, the Emergency and the Japanese occupation during World War II were events that happened generations ago and are mere 'stories' to the young. At the time of writing, it has been just over five years since MH370 vanished, and many are still moved by its mere mention.

For Martin Vengadesan personally, the situation was one of initial disbelief. He was woken up on his day off by a call from a colleague. "Have you guys put up the list of passengers on the missing plane?" his colleague asked.

"Not sure what's going on, I'll have to check," Martin replied.

Five minutes and many WhatsApp messages later, Martin was scrambling out of the shower and into his clothes, car, and into *The Star* office, where he was one of those manning the online desk. In fact, it was his first week as the senior editor on the desk. This was big.

The days that followed are still clear in Martin's mind. Even as news broke, there was a flurry of conflicting reports. A MAS plane en route to Beijing had dropped off the radar over the South China Sea. Then there were false sightings; some claimed the plane had landed in China, others that smoke was seen near Vietnam, Interpol had spotted Iranian hijackers. And so it began.

In the weeks after the disappearance of the 227 passengers and 12 crew members, Martin and his colleagues barely slept, always hoping to be woken by the news that the plane, which had inexplicably changed course and vanished from communication lines, had been found. There were so many times when false hope was raised. But every new crackpot theory was debunked soon after it was mooted.

People came to the office waving printouts of satellite images claiming they had found the plane. Colleagues claimed the Indonesians had spotted it. People in the Maldives had seen it. Radio and television stations from around the world were trying to call them about it, many with their own agenda. In fact, when they were interviewed by the foreign media, the media sometimes seemed to be trying to trip them up, as if they were part of some cover-up. Their job was to stay calm and alert.

But in their hearts, they knew that 48 hours was the cut-off point, beyond which it was unreasonable to hope for a safe and simple solution. When that time frame passed, the horrible reality slowly started sinking in. Each and every fact was startling. Nothing really made sense.

The Boeing 777 took off from Kuala Lumpur at 12:41am on March 8, bound for Beijing. It vanished from Malaysian civilian radar at 1:30am, just before passing to Vietnamese air traffic control. Communications on board had been switched off. It blipped on military radars until 2:15am, but that sighting was only later identified as flight MH370.

Reports were confusing from the start. The Vietnamese seemed to have spotted oil slicks in the South China Sea, but other sources indicated the plane had performed a U-turn and flew past Indonesia and in the direction of the Indian Ocean.

Suspicion fell in turn on Uighur terrorists, trafficked Iranians, even the Americans at the mysterious base of Diego Garcia, but nothing was concrete. Could it have been a technical fault? Dozens of nations were soon sending ships and planes to look for MH370 as part of a Joint Investigation Team but to no avail.

Temperatures rose. False sightings abounded. There was a farcical misstep when a *bomoh* was hired to track down the plane. There was even a hideous attempt to make a blockbuster movie out of it. And in a move of almost unbelievable heartlessness, some of the missing people had their bank accounts cleared out by unscrupulous bank officers.

Bank officer Nur Shila Kanan and her mechanic husband Basheer Ahmad Maula Sahul Hameed deservedly received hefty jail sentences of eight and seven years, respectively, for the crime of stealing RM77,530 from the bank accounts of four people who were on that flight.

Many of those on the flight were Chinese nationals, and their relatives were mistrustful of the Malaysian government. Families of those on board were understandably distraught. The hurtful conspiracy theories didn't help either.

Some attacked the captain of the plane, Captain Zaharie Ahmad Shah, which angered his friend, Peter Chong, who also happened to be Martin's friend. Chong told Martin that he felt that if there was any element of foul play in the form of a hijacking, then Zaharie would have been a victim of it.

"Zaharie is someone who is very passionate about flying and very aware of the great responsibility a pilot bears towards his passengers and crew. He is a management pilot, which means he doesn't just fly but is involved in training and examining other pilots. He took it very seriously and we used to joke that he is one of the lucky people who has made his job his hobby. He is a good man and humble despite his senior position as a pilot. He wanted to make a difference to the community."

Chong was outraged by allegations implicating Zaharie in the disappearance of the flight — pilot suicide or otherwise. "I think sometimes the media forgets about the human element; the emotions of the families involved.

How can you irresponsibly cast such accusations on a man whose family is grieving and worried about his safety?"

The nation was united in grief on March 24, 2014, when then Prime Minister Najib Abdul Razak sadly announced that MH370 had probably ended up in the Indian Ocean. There was still no conclusion and the hunger for an answer to all the questions remained undiminished. In fact, the pressure to backtrack on that announcement was intense.

On January 29, 2015, the Department of Civil Aviation Director-General Azharuddin Abdul Rahman declared the disappearance an accident and that all aboard were presumed dead. Although this was done for legal purposes, the search for the missing place would continue.

Finally, more than four years after the plane went missing, newly appointed Transport Minister Anthony Loke announced that the search for the plane would be called off. The final day of the search was May 29, 2018. The company engaged in the final stage of looking for the plane's wreckage was Houston-based Ocean Infinity, which was searching on a 'no find, no fee' basis.

VERDICT There is no clear cut explanation as to what happened, and we may have to face the fact that there might never be one.

37

THE DOWNING OF MH17

Date : July 17, 2014
Crime : Four months after one Malaysia Airlines plane goes
missing, another is shot down from the sky

Details: It was the very worst sort of *deja vu*. Martin
Vengadesan had just left the office and was pulling into a
petrol station when the message came through. Another
MAS plane down. Another incredulous call. Another mad
scramble.

He and his colleagues were numb with disbelief, yet they
reacted almost as if they had got used to it. But who could
really get used to another tragic loss of life? Just as he had
done a few months earlier, Martin had a full work day with
the midnight to 8am shift on the night of the crisis because
he couldn't tear himself away from what was unfolding.

This time there was very little mystery. The people in
the plane had been shot out of the sky. Murdered.

Flight MH17 had departed Amsterdam at 12:15pm
(7:15pm Malaysian time) carrying 283 passengers and 15

crew members. It was scheduled to arrive at Kuala Lumpur International Airport at 6:10am (Malaysian time) the next day. It never did.

Somewhere over the Ukraine, the flight lost contact with Ukrainian air traffic control. Despite assurances that the route it was travelling on was safe, the MAS flight was shot down in a war-torn zone, caught between pro-Russian Ukrainian separatists and the Ukraine government. It soon became very clear that there were no survivors.

The majority of those on board were from the Netherlands and the dead included 43 Malaysians. As we scanned the wires for pictures, we saw bodies in a field, some still strapped to their seats. These were pictures to break your heart.

In this case, Malaysia was able to react quickly. Prime Minister Najib Abdul Razak and our top officials reached an understanding with Alexander Borodai, leader of the separatist Donetsk People's Republic where the tragedy occurred. Against a backdrop of international tensions, Malaysia did what it could to bring the bodies home.

Were Martin and his colleagues angry? Yes. There was even a boy on the plane who was the nephew of a former colleague. They had seen pictures of him as a toddler. The boy's grandmother had called *The Star* to say that her daughter, son-in-law and three grandchildren were on board the plane. Now Martin and his colleagues were looking at pictures of Marnix van den Hende as a 12-year-old victim of this horrendous crime.

Malaysia obtained custody of the black box and got an agreement for independent international investigators to be given access to the crash site. Malaysia worked with Dutch and British authorities for the best forensic analyses possible.

Hearts were aching. Malaysia called for a cessation of hostilities at the crash site and a policing of the area. Compensation was discussed. There was talk of the United Nations treating the downing of the plane as a war crime. The Malaysian Government rightly declared a Day of National Mourning on August 22 to honour the victims.

Patrick Lee, then a reporter with *The Star*, was flown to the scene of the tragedy. Four years on, he recalled just what an unusual set of circumstances it was.

"The mood was varied depending on the place you went to. In July of 2014, the fighting in the eastern part of Ukraine had been raging for a bit, and there was this feeling in the air that there was a conflict going on in the country. From my point of view, you got the sense that there were two sides to the country: one being pro-Ukraine, and the other being pro-Russia.

"In a word, it was surreal. When we look at media reports or videos of war zones, or war movies, some of us may seem to think that a lot of these conflict zones are constant battlefields where gun battles rage non-stop and all semblance of society comes to a halt."

But the reality that Lee encountered was somewhat different. "Donetsk was a beautiful city, with running infrastructure: water, electricity, trains, cars, shops, petrol stations and restaurants. There were people walking their dogs near the very pretty parks in the main city, and outside of it, people taking buses, tending to their homes. All the usual things people might be doing if there wasn't a conflict happening. Heck, one of the guys I met there was even taking his driving exam!"

Despite this, there were telling signs of a silent war. "The city and many of the towns were empty. Ghost towns. It was probably ten percent full, and I was told that many people fled the conflict to go somewhere else where there wasn't any fighting. And every now and then you'd see tanks rolling down the streets, and armed fighters in military garb. Then there'd be the rumbles of artillery or rockets in the distance, plumes of smoke rising from burning buildings or sites far away, and at one point in the countryside, jets flying overhead."

Everywhere Lee went, he met people who understood the impact of what had happened.

"Many people were very curious when they found out that (photographer) Kamarul Arrifin and I were Malaysians. They definitely knew what we were there for, but I don't think many of them had met a Malaysian until we arrived. Most people were quite friendly, even accommodating, once they knew where we came from."

Despite that, Lee's time in the region brought him no closer to getting answers as to who was directly responsible for downing the plane. "There were a lot of fingers pointed, but nobody in eastern Ukraine thought that the

Russians, the Donbass fighters or whoever were there, were responsible for the shootdown. I never met any of the suspects, whoever they were."

Lee himself knew one person aboard the downed flight. "I know one person who was killed. The actress Shuba Jay who died along with her husband and daughter. I wasn't close to her but we met a few times because we happened to be in the same circles of friends at the time. I never met her family, but I can tell you that her friends were crushed by her death."

Lee found himself comparing the two ill-fated flights. "With MH370, there was no plane, no wreckage to look at. Only press conferences, officials and the passengers' next of kin. A lot of questions and very few answers. A general sense of confusion. But with MH17, there were a couple of times where it was kind of overwhelming.

"That came with seeing the wreckage, smelling the mix of burnt jet fuel and decomposing human remains, seeing strewn belongings and clothes, the Hari Raya greeting cards, and meeting crying locals who came across the bodies of the victims, and telling you the state in which they found them. At some point some even saw them falling in large numbers from the sky.

"I don't think I'll ever forget what I saw there."

But what justice will there be for the victims of MH17? Who will be called to trial? The Donetsk rebels who are believed to have callously shot down the plane of innocents? Well, they blame the Ukrainian government. Some tried to implicate Russian President Vladimir Putin. Much of the testimony and evidence strongly suggests it was ill-disciplined separatists who shot down the plane on a lark.

Finally, on May 25, 2018, nearly four years after the plane was shot down, a probe carried out by prosecutors from Malaysia, the Netherlands, Australia, Belgium and Ukraine laid the blame squarely on Russia. "It is the first time the finger points to one specific country," said Dutch Prime Minister Mark Rutte. "We are holding Russia responsible for their role in the deployment on the Buk rocket system. Russia didn't cooperate with the international legal requests in relation to the investigation."

Nonetheless, the Netherlands and its partners informed Russia that it expected full assistance and the investigation is in the final stages of identifying perpetrators who will be tried under Dutch law.

On June 19, 2019, Dutch prosecutors announced that three Russian nationals and a Ukrainian would be tried on murder charges for their alleged roles in bringing down the plane.

The Joint Investigative Team said that evidence showed a direct line of military command between Moscow and pro-Russia separatists fighting in eastern Ukraine. They played phone calls of the suspects discussing the incident by telephone, via social media chats and a computer image reconstruction of the events.

The suspects were named as Igor Girkin, Sergei Dubinsky, Oleg Pulatov and Leonid Kharchenko.

"We will send out international arrest warrants for the four suspects that we will prosecute," Dutch chief prosecutor Fred Westerbeke said, adding that their trial is expected to commence in March 2020 in the Netherlands.

In August 2019, before the commencement of the trial, Malaysia's Prime Minister Dr Mahathir Mohamad expressed doubts over the Joint Investigative Team's findings, saying there was not enough evidence to blame Russia for the shooting.

VERDICT The trail of evidence points unerringly at Russian involvement in the shooting.

38

PAEDOPHILE NIGHTMARE

Date : December 19, 2014
Crime : A British man is arrested leading to the exposure of his serial child molestation and pornography, most of it carried out in Malaysia

Details: On the face of it, Richard Huckle was a nice young man. A former grammar school boy from Ashford, Kent, he had backpacked around the world and volunteered with Christian communities that worked with the underprivileged. While in Malaysia, he was even featured in a promotional video that was part of a British Council campaign.

But behind Huckle's gentle demeanour lay a monstrous appetite. He was hiding behind a mask of false religious sentiment for the purpose of gaining access to children. In particular, he would target orphans and neglected children from broken homes.

Were it not for an investigation by Australian authorities, Huckle might have continued to get away with his vile

British national, Richard Huckle (social media photo).

crimes. He was in the habit of posting photographs of the abuse of boys and girls on the darknet, on a website called True Love Zone (TLZ), where paedophiles shared their sickening tales of 'conquests'.

Australian investigators posing as paedophiles gained access to this world and were horrified by what they encountered. They tipped off the British police who intercepted Huckle at London's Gatwick Airport upon his return to the UK from Malaysia for the Christmas holidays.

In Huckle's possession were a heavily-encrypted laptop computer and camera. They contained over 20,000 images depicting child sex abuse. Over 1,000 of the photographs showed Huckle himself committing a variety of sexual offences including rape.

The laptop contained a ledger in which he detailed the abuse of 191 victims.

After sifting through the evidence, police laid 91 charges including that of rape against 23 children he had groomed while posing as a volunteer working with Christian communities in the Malaysian capital. His victims were aged between six months and 12 years, and the offences were committed between 2006 and 2014.

So just how did he gain access to so many victims? Well, Huckle targeted poor areas where churches carried out social work. Once he had gained access to the community, he would do odd jobs, often posing as a camera expert. He always seemed willing to spend more time with children whom others didn't have time for. Perhaps the fact that he was Caucasian helped him to get his foot in the door more easily and have his authority unchallenged.

The communities that Huckle preyed on were not hundreds of kilometres away from urban Kuala Lumpur, but right in the heart of it. To protect the identity of his victims, the communities and churches he was involved with shall remain unnamed.

His own words reveal him to be a strange mixture of revolting pervert and someone who tried to convince himself that there was affection and mutual attraction between himself and the children he was manipulating and molesting.

"I'd hit the jackpot, a three-year-old girl as loyal to me as my dog and nobody seemed to care," he once wrote. On another occasion, he bragged about the ability to compare the bodies of the same 'lover' even as she aged from five to 12 years old. He also gloated that 'impoverished kids are definitely much easier to seduce than middle-class Western kids'.

Huckle even wrote a guide to child abuse and contemplated publishing it for profit!

Eventually, British Judge Peter Rook handed Richard Huckle 23 life sentences to be served concurrently after he pleaded guilty to 71 counts of child sex offences. That's 71 out of the original 91 charges.

"Relentlessly you preyed on the very young," said Rook. "You targeted and groomed impoverished children." Huckle's crimes touched a raw nerve in a UK reeling from the repeated exposure of sexual crimes against children committed by BBC celebrities like Jimmy Saville, Rolf Harris, Gary Glitter and Jonathan King.

Huckle tried to plead in mitigation that his victims did not suffer pain. It was justifiably dismissed.

In a letter of remorse read out in court, the deluded Huckle said, "I completely misjudged the affections I received from these children. My low self-esteem and lack of confidence with women was no excuse to be using these children as an outlet."

He also blamed others saying that he was easily influenced into carrying out these heinous crimes.

"Thank God the Australian and British police got involved to stop this monster," said a source who covered the case. "This is exactly the kind of case that could go unpunished in Malaysia for many years, and indeed it did! There's no political will and no technical savvy to take the time to go undercover and expose these horrific crimes.

You wonder too if the victims are going to get proper counselling because the mentality among the community is more about denial that the events happened and covering up because of the shame it brings.

"Even today, the location of Huckle's crimes is hushed up to prevent exposure of the victims, but it also means that it is easier for the community to sweep things under the carpet. We are not confronting what really happened."

As is often the case with those who commit sexual crimes against children, Huckle was not able to escape another form of justice – doled out by a fellow prisoner.

On October 13, 2019, having spent less than five years behind bars, he was found dead in his cell in Full Sutton Prison, Yorkshire. He had been stabbed to death with a makeshift knife and a fellow prisoner was held in connection with the murder.

According to the UK's *The Sun* newspaper, Huckle was not just stabbed. He had been strangled with a guitar string, and condoms and pens had been shoved down his throat. A gory end to an unforgivable life.

VERDICT A vile criminal who committed unspeakable crimes against children was locked up, and then murdered in an extrajudicial killing. We cannot condone this form of justice, but few will mourn his death.

39

TRAFFICKING TORMENT

Date : May 13, 2015
Crime : In the heart of the jungles of Perlis, over 100 bodies
are found in clandestine camps

Details: Wang Kelian is a small town in the sleepy northern state of Perlis. Located near the Malaysia-Thailand border crossing, it was never as well known as the other intersections at Padang Besar and Golok.

That changed on May 13, 2015, when Malaysian police reported a gruesome discovery of horrifying proportions. No less than 139 graves of human trafficking victims were found in 28 detention camps strewn across the jungles in the border region. Most of the dead were believed to be members of Myanmar's displaced Rohingya community.

As the world's media descended upon the remote sites, disbelieving Malaysians asked themselves how such a thing had come to pass. How was it that Malaysia had become such a haven for human traffickers?

The answer lies in a confluence of factors. The first is

that Malaysia's multi-ethnic population makes it an ideal place for trafficked labourers from all parts of Asia to blend in.

The second is that our porous borders are easily penetrated by trafficking syndicates. It's no coincidence that from 1993 until April 2015, Malaysia and Thailand practised a free-flow zone, which allowed people from both countries to move freely between Wang Prachan in Thailand and Wang Kelian for shopping, without travel documents. This policy clearly played an enabling role in Wang Kelian's development as a human trafficking centre.

The third factor is lax law enforcement, with immigration and police officials often being willing and compliant partners in this criminal endeavour. The fact that trafficking victims are generally faceless and stateless makes them all the more vulnerable to abuses of power.

Former news reporter Christine Cheah was among the hordes of journalists flown up from Kuala Lumpur in the immediate aftermath of the discoveries.

"I made two trips to Wang Kelian totalling about a week. The first trip was when the camps had just been discovered in May 2015. Foreign reporters rushed there as did the local press. We were asked to wait for police who had set up camp at a valley at the base of a hill. Then we were led into the jungle."

Cheah was struck by its proximity to civilisation. "It was a route near the main road, maybe half an hour away. You could see that the jungle trek has been trod many times, day in and day out.

Jungle camps at Wang Kelian (photo by Christine Cheah).

"That's the thing about going to abandoned camps. What do you see there? Everything is destroyed, from food waste, torn down tents, and rusty nails and fences. And in your mind you start to piece things together."

The camps were a quarter of the size of a football field. At first, the media were taken to just two out of the many camps, but Cheah was exposed to bigger revelations on her second trip.

"We saw enough cleared ground for helicopters to land. And just after that were the graves.

"There were 20 empty graves in a straight line. Some just a few feet long that must have held the bodies of children. It looked like what I had read and seen of Vietnamese war camps. There was barbed wire and a high watch tower to survey the area. There were also confined areas looking like they were used for solitary confinement.

"I freaked out when I saw the remnants of a human skull. Finding a child's slipper confirmed that little children must have lived, and probably died there. The small cages made me sad. You know it was not meant for chickens or other livestock."

Cheah also saw generators for electricity supply, play areas and changing areas. There was even a well-constructed bridge over a lake in what was probably the most recently inhabited camp.

"It was an eerie feeling looking at the deserted camp and especially the unmarked deserted graves. These were all Rohingyas looking for a better life. At that point I felt like I was surrounded by signs of human misery. At one point standing in the jungle, I just found myself imagining how lonely it must have been at night."

Autopsies that were conducted on the corpses found that the victims had either starved to death or died from diseases. Aside from neglect and malnutrition, the likelihood that some had died from abuse was high, particularly as traffickers were known to demand 'ransoms' from family members of victims, and would beat the victims with hammers should the sums of money fail to be paid.

When looking for answers, Cheah and her fellow reporters were stymied at every turn. "We did try to question the police who had led us to the camps but they didn't really follow us around. It did seem like they must have known about it.

"Similarly, we wanted to interview the people around the area. But we realised that they probably knew about the camps but turned a blind eye to them. The Rohingya would not necessarily have blended in with the locals, who were of a Malay/Thai ethnic mix.

"We also went to Thailand and interviewed a guy who was a translator for the Rohingya. He said he helped people to escape and he had nice stories to recount but our reservation was that he might well have been helping those who did the trafficking."

One of the questions that cropped up was the destruction of the camps, which was ordered by the local police themselves. The explanation given was that the camps were destroyed to prevent further use by human trafficking rings, but surely as crime scenes they should have been thoroughly investigated by forensics experts? Was the haste to destroy the camps part of a cover-up?

Reports also emerged that the Perlis police had first stumbled upon the camps in January 2015 but only decided to expose them to the outside world more than four months later. They had no choice once *Malay Mail* journalists S Arulldas and Mohd Sayuti Zainudin exposed the camp.

Considering that the trafficking camps had been in operation for a few years, and that more than 100 people had lost their lives, precious little by way of prosecution has taken place since.

After initially trying to focus investigations on the immigration department, 12 police officers were arrested for possible involvement in the case but in March 2017, then Deputy Prime Minister Ahmad Zahid Hamidi said all

Human skulls found at Wang Kelian (photo by Christine Cheah).

12 had been released due to insufficient evidence.

The only positive prosecutions to emerge were clearly that of small-time operators. Two Myanmar teenagers were each sentenced to three years in jail, a Thai man got five years and a Bangladeshi was jailed for 10 years in 2016. The Bangladeshi, Nurul Islam, who burst into tears upon sentencing in June 2016, claimed that he had been beaten repeatedly until he agreed to carry out the trafficking work.

Despite calls for an RCI into the event, the case appeared to be slipping into the history books without any significant prosecution. However, following a change of government, one was finally set up with the consent of the Yang di-Pertuan Agong on January 29, 2019, to review the cases. The inquiry is ongoing and chaired by former Chief Justice Ariffin Zakaria.

VERDICT Over 100 human trafficking victims died in the jungle, and it remains to be seen if the perpetrators will be called to book.

40

THE DICTATOR'S BROTHER

Date : February 13, 2017
Crime : A North Korean man dies suddenly at a Malaysian
         airport, triggering an international showdown

Details: It happened in a crowded airport terminal. An act
so swift and surprising one would barely have caught it
even if looking out for it. A casually-dressed Macau-bound
Korean traveller named Kim Chol was accosted at the KLIA
departure lounge by two women working in tandem.

Seemingly randomly, one of them wiped an oily
substance on his face before the other approached him
from behind and covered his eyes and mouth with her
hands. Both women quickly strode away, the damage done.

As CCTV footage reveals, the distressed Korean
approaches airport staff for help. They try their best but
his demise is swift. At first it's just anxiety, but within two
hours he had a seizure and stopped breathing.

The substance that killed him was a compound version
of VX — also known as O-ethyl S-diisopropylaminomethyl

Kim Jong-nam with his father in 1981 (North Korean News Agency).

methylphosphonothiolate — classified by the United Nations as a weapon of mass destruction and banned by the Chemical Weapons Convention of 1993. North Korea, which did not ratify the Convention, is suspected of holding a stockpile.

Pure VX would have killed its handler and it is believed that the two separate substances combined chemically on his face to create a fatal dose.

The dead man was travelling under the assumed name Kim Chol. He was, however, soon revealed to be Kim Jong-nam, the eldest son of the late North Korean dictator Kim Jong-il and the grandson of the regime's founder Kim Il-sung. He was once tipped to take up 'succession' of the warped so-called communist state, but after schooling in Europe, he showed no interest in political power.

Jong-il's older son fell fatally out of favour when he was arrested in 2001 attempting to enter Japan using a false passport. His main purpose had been to visit Tokyo

Disneyland. Despite showing no interest in challenging his younger half-brother Kim Jong-un for the 'throne', he was a marked man who had survived at least two previous attempts on his life.

The two women who had smeared the substance on Jong-nam were Indonesian Siti Aisyah and Vietnamese Doan Thị Huong. Both were quickly apprehended by the police. They told the barely credible story that they had been recruited to take part in what they thought was a prank TV show.

They claimed that they were themselves victims, tricked into becoming inadvertent assassins, in what they alleged was an elaborate plot by a group of North Korean agents. Chillingly, four North Vietnamese agents — going by the names of Hong Song-hac, Rhi Ji-hyon, O Jong-gil and Ri Jae-nam — were also in the vicinity when the attack occurred. They were believed to have been standing by with a back-up plan to finish Jong-nam off in the event that the VX failed to do the trick. Once they realised it had succeeded, they hopped on to pre-booked flights out of Malaysia.

A reporter assigned to cover the case said that it was hard not to feel sorry for Kim Jong-nam. "It's sad to watch the grainy footage of the attack. He is asking for help and then his final moments with a seizure and being treated medically. He knew his life was suddenly under grievous threat but couldn't figure a way out in time.

"To me it also showed how heartless and sinister the North Korean rogue state really is. People try to make Kim Jong-un out to be a figure of fun, but he's really a brutal military dictator sitting on a stockpile of nuclear weapons. He was prepared to eliminate his own half-brother who was clearly not interested in challenging his rule and just wanted to go about his own life."

However, what unfolded further showed that North Korea was prepared to be absolutely ruthless and show no respect for Malaysia's sovereignty and rule of law.

On February 28, the North Korean government dispatched a high-level delegation to Malaysia.

They rubbished the claim that VX nerve agent was used to kill one of its citizens, claiming that it smacked of a false accusation cooked up by the United States and South Korea. They falsely claimed that the death was caused by a 'heart attack'.

On March 4, the North Korean ambassador Kang Chol, who had been aggressively leading the campaign of misinformation as if his life depended on it (and it probably did), was declared *persona non grata* by Malaysia and given 48 hours to leave the country. He had been told to apologise for making claims that Malaysia was conspiring with South Korea in investigating the assassination.

"The statements I've made are an expression of the righteous stand as ambassador of the Democratic Republic of North Korea in this country on the pre-targeted investigation by the Malaysian police.

"They have conducted Jong-nam's autopsy without the consent or attendance of the DPRK embassy and later arrested a DPRK citizen (believed to be the chemist behind the blending of substances to create the fatal compound) without any clear evidence showing his involvement in the incident," Kang Chol told the press via a translator.

The North Koreans retaliated by dismissing Malaysia's ambassador to Pyongyang. Tensions escalated on March 6, when Malaysia announced the cancellation of visa-free entry for North Koreans, citing security issues.

North Korea proceeded to up the ante with a travel ban on all Malaysians in Pyongyang, trapping three diplomats and six family members. Malaysian authorities then imposed reciprocal measures, prohibiting North Korean citizens from leaving Malaysia.

The impasse only ended on March 30, when Malaysia agreed to hand over Jong-nam's corpse and send three North Koreans wanted for questioning back to North Korea.

Eddie Chua, who had made a strange habit of holidaying in North Korea on no less than three occasions in the years preceding the murder, said he decided to put a swift end to that practice!

The true vile nature of the North Korean rogue state was exposed in its treatment of Otto Warmbier, an American college student who was sentenced to 15 years hard labour in March 2016 for the crime of stealing a propaganda poster. Shortly after his sentencing in March 2016, he suffered a severe neurological injury and fell into a coma. In June 2017, he was released by North Korea in a vegetative state and died soon after.

Aishah and Doan, meanwhile, were arraigned to stand trial for murder, facing the mandatory death sentence if convicted under section 302 of the Penal Code. The trial commenced on October 2, 2017.

There was an interesting technicality when chemical weapons expert Raja Subramaniam testified in court that the Malaysian lab where the VX sample was tested was not among centres designated by the Organisation for the Prohibition of Chemical Weapons (OPCW). But by and large, the feeling was that those on trial were the 'mules' and not the 'kingpins' behind the murder.

On August 16, 2018, the court ordered Siti Aisyah and Doan to enter their defence on the charge of murdering Jong-nam.

However, observers were stunned on March 12, 2019, when Siti Aisyah was released. High Court judge Justice Azmi Ariffin gave her a discharge not amounting to an acquittal after the Prosecution withdrew the charge against Siti Aisyah without furnishing any reason.

Deputy Public Prosecutor Muhamad Iskandar Ahmad merely withdrew the charge against her in accordance with section 254(1) of the Criminal Procedure Code.

The Indonesian embassy then revealed that ever since Siti Aisyah's arrest, Indonesia's President Joko Widodo (Jokowi) had called for coordination between relevant authorities, including his foreign minister, police chief, attorney general and head of intelligence, to press for her release.

It said the efforts to release Siti Aisyah was reportedly made in a series of meetings, including one between Jokowi and Prime Minister Dr Mahathir Mohamad at the

Kim Jong-nam's brother, North Korean leader Kim Jong-un (North Korean News Agency, 2014).

Bogor Presidential Palace in West Java, Indonesia, on June 29, 2018.

Her shock release was followed a couple of months later by the announcement that Doan had been sentenced to three years and four months in jail by the Shah Alam High Court after pleading guilty to a new charge under section 324 of the Penal Code for voluntarily causing hurt by dangerous weapons or means.

She was entitled to a one-third remission on the prison sentence, which was ordered to run from the date of her arrest, and shockingly just a week after the announcement, on May 3, 2019, she was freed from Kajang Prison and flown home to Vietnam.

Within two-and-a-half years of his cruel murder, all of Jong-nam's killers were free. Clearly, Malaysia had decided to make diplomatic gestures of goodwill to both Indonesia and Vietnam, and there was even talk about the eventual reopening of the Malaysian embassy in North Korea.

The masterminds completely escaped prosecution and the foot soldiers who carried out the crime served less than 30 months behind bars.

VERDICT In a case that was all about international politics, nobody in Malaysia showed the political will to advocate justice for the murdered man.

41

THE PASTOR'S ABDUCTION

Date : February 13, 2017
Crime : A religious activist is forced from his car in broad
daylight and has not been seen since

Details: On the very same day that a North Korean man
(later revealed to be the brother of dictator Kim Jong-
un) met with a mysterious death at KLIA, a pastor went
missing.

Pastor Raymond Koh was taken on the morning of
February 13, 2017, in Kelana Jaya, Selangor, by a group of
men covered from head to toe in black and driving black
SUVs and motorcycles. The men surrounded his vehicle
and a struggle ensued, during which the windscreen of
the car was smashed. The men forced Koh into one of
their cars. This brazen abduction in broad daylight on a
relatively busy road was captured by CCTV cameras and the
footage went viral.

However, as weeks went by and there was no sign of the
pastor, conspiracy theories began to emerge. Candlelight

vigils were held to support the family and questions were asked about the commitment of the police in the investigation.

It was also theorised that Koh's disappearance was linked to accusations that he preached Christianity to Muslims in the northern state of Perlis, in clear violation of the law. Another theory was that a human trafficking syndicate was behind his abduction.

What was most alarming was the possible tie-in between the disappearance of Koh and the disappearances of social activist Amri Che Mat in Perlis as well as Pastor Joshua Hilmy and his wife Ruth Sitepu, all of whom vanished in November 2016.

Amri had driven his SUV out from his Kangar home close to midnight on November 24, 2016, and his vehicle was later found at a construction site near the Bukit Cabang Sports School. Amri was linked to the spread of Shia Islam, which is also illegal in Sunni Islam Malaysia.

Joshua Hilmy was believed to have converted to Christianity from Islam. He and his wife were both Christian preachers and were last seen on November 30, 2016, at their home in Selangor. A missing persons report, however, was only filed on March 6, 2017. When viewed together, the disappearances appear to be linked.

With Koh's family citing a lack of feedback from the police and a seeming lack of conviction in pursuing genuine leads, public pressure led the Human Rights Commission of Malaysia (Suhakam) to carry out its own inquiry into the disappearances.

"There was definitely something odd," said a reporter who covered the inquiry. "The police investigation seemed to be more about whether or not Pastor Koh was proselytising rather than his disappearance. Even getting the CCTV footage was done by Koh's children and not the police. It was the family who went around getting information. They identified the crime scene based on the police description and obtained CCTV footage from several houses nearby. That's shocking."

The reporter said another curiosity was that the car did not belong to the missing man, and that it was the car owner who called Koh's family to inform them that something had happened. "An eyewitness called the police. A chambering student called Roeshan Celestine Gomez had seen the whole abduction and he initially thought it was a movie shoot! He then went to make a police report."

Gomez also claimed that the investigating officer told him that the modus operandi sounded like a police operation. Gomez's friend had tried to film the abduction on her phone but was warned not to do so by one of the masked men. "The owner of the car, who was then in Sabah, got a call from the police following Gomez's report and he was the one who informed Koh's family of the disappearance," said the reporter.

In January 2018, part-time driver Lam Chang Nam was charged in connection with Pastor Koh's disappearance. Lam was originally charged in March 2017 with extorting RM30,000 from Koh's son Jonathan to release his father. However, some 10 months later, he was charged with kidnap. The police issued a statement indicating that they were looking for seven others.

Koh's wife Susanna Liew claimed that the timing of Lam's charge seemed to be an attempt to prevent the inquiry from proceeding as it occurred after Lam had been arrested for many months and just a day before the inquiry resumed. "If he really is involved, then he should know where Raymond is now. Bring him out and let the perpetrators be apprehended and justice served," she said.

Suhakam then suspended its independent investigation of the case after being notified that Lam had been charged, as required by law.

Malaysian police continued to maintain that these cases were being investigated as 'missing persons' and not abductions with no link established between the disappearances so far. An NGO called Citizens Against Enforced Disappearances (CAGED) was even formed in the wake of these abductions.

The inquiry then focused on Amri's disappearance and with the change of government on May 9, 2018, came a new development. Amri's wife Norhayati Mohd Ariffin made a police report in Shah Alam claiming a sergeant from the Special Branch in Perlis had come to her house on May 12 to give her new information about the abduction of Amri and Koh. The informer allegedly said the men had been taken by a team from Bukit Aman. However, when called by the inquiry, he denied making such a statement.

The reporter said: "I think Pastor Koh knew that he was

doing something dangerous. A few years before on August 3, 2011, he organised an event at the Damansara Utama Methodist Church and it was raided by Jais (the Selangor Islamic Religious Department) who found 12 Muslims present. He was also sent two bullets as a warning after that raid."

A note that accompanied the bullets referenced the killing of former Lunas assemblyman Dr Joe Fernandez, who was shot dead on November 4, 2000, by a pillion rider on a motorcycle when he stopped at a traffic junction in Bukit Mertajam. Dr Fernandez had been targeted in a smear campaign accusing him of helping Muslims convert to Christianity.

The reporter adds: "In Amri's case also, the police have admitted that they were monitoring him and Perlis Hope came under attack from those who said it's linked to Shia."

While there were differing views as to the extent of the links between the cases, the reporter was in little doubt. "Personally, I think they are linked. There are similarities about the modus operandi under which the abductions were carried out. I think having listened to the testimony of the wives of Koh and Amri, I think they are pretty solid. Sometimes they may get facts wrong, but I don't see why they would lie. Also the police in both cases were very bad at giving answers and repeatedly contradicted themselves."

Given the perceived attempts to suppress the case, it was quite a stunner when the reconvened Suhakam inquiry delivered its verdict on April 3, 2019. In no uncertain terms, the inquiry panel announced that Koh and Amri were victims of 'enforced disappearance by state agents'. The police's own Special Branch, no less!

Suhakam commissioner Mah Weng Kwai said that an inquiry panel of himself, Professor Dr Aishah Bidin and Dr Nik Salida Suhaila Nik Saleh reached the unanimous conclusion after lengthy discussions.

"There is direct and circumstantial evidence which proves, on a balance of probabilities, that he was abducted by state agents, by Special Branch, Bukit Aman," he said when announcing the findings of the public inquiry.

The uproar was immediate and warranted. It was a chilling confirmation that Malaysia was a police state. The loud call to turn Suhakam's findings into a criminal trial still had to wait though. Soon after the verdict, Home Minister Muhyiddin Yassin announced that a special task force would be appointed to look into the case.

However, when he announced the composition of the task force on June 26, 2019, it led to another controversy. Headed by former High Court judge Abdul Rahim Uda, the team was to comprise Royal Malaysian Police Legal Unit Chief Mokhtar Mohd Noor, police Integrity and Standard Compliance Department Director Zamri Yahya, Director of Enforcement Agency Integrity Commission Operations Muhammad Bukhari Abdul Hamid, and Mohd Sophian Zakaria, a legal officer from the Attorney General's Chambers' Prosecution division. Mohd Russaini Idrus, who is secretary of the Police Force Commission, was appointed the task force's secretary.

The inclusion of Mokhtar was particularly criticised on

the basis of conflict of interest, while in general, the team had the look of old regime insiders instead of independent investigators. It didn't help that all of them were Malay-Muslim males with a history of service within the state apparatus.

"I am confident that the special task force will be able to carry out their duty to look into the matter. I expect to get a report on their findings in six months and leave it to them to determine who to call in the process of their investigation," said the oblivious Muhyiddin in announcing the team.

Koh's family was less than impressed, pointing out that there were no women in the task force and adding that it did not reflect the composition and the multiracial spirit of the country. Norhayati expressed unhappiness over Mokhtar's inclusion, saying that his unit was 'implicated in the flawed investigation into Amri's abduction and later, in the team representing the police during the Suhakam inquiry'.

"Mokhtar is clearly an interested party and so represents a conflict of interest," she said.

Mokhtar stepped down within a few days of his appointment to be replaced by two men, Azian Umar from the Malaysian Anti-Corruption Commission (MACC) and lawyer Roger Tan. It remains to be seen what direction the task force will take in its investigation but some difficult questions have to be asked, for in the end, where are Koh, Amri and the others who were abducted?

The reporter who covered the inquiry said: "As more and more time goes by, we will have to accept that they are probably not going to be found alive and well. Could they have been disposed of by the same people who had abducted them? What sort of motive could possibly justify such drastic repercussions?"

VERDICT Enforced disappearance at the hands of state agents from the Special Branch is just about as damning as it gets, but will we ever see a criminal trial?

42

THE MYSTERIOUS EPIDEMIC

Date : May 2019
Crime : 15 Bateq villagers in a remote part of Kelantan fall
prey to a mystery illness

Details: This story begins in early June when reports of a number of deaths, estimated to be around eight to 10 within a month, first surfaced on a Facebook post by NGO Sahabat Jariah.

This NGO, working with the Orang Asli, highlighted that a number of villagers from the Bateq tribe living in the remote outpost of Kampung Kuala Koh in Gua Musang, Kelantan, had died of a mysterious disease.

Martin Vengadesan was alerted to it by an activist working in Sungai Berua, Terengganu, but attempts to verify the news met with little or no response. Given that it was so far away, it was easy to push it out of one's mind.

Then another NGO Klima Action Malaysia announced a donation drive, saying it was planning to drop off food, fresh water and medical supplies to the stricken village.

All of a sudden, on June 9, news broke nationally when Minister in the Prime Minister's Department P Waythamoorthy flew to Gua Musang. His aide Andrew Sagayam, on his first week on the job, confirmed to the media that there had been 14 deaths in the village since early May.

Kampung Kuala Koh was soon cordoned off to outsiders and declared a red zone. Kelantan Health Director Dr Zaini Hussin said the move was to curtail the spread of pneumonia infections that could be transmitted through respiration. The Health Ministry announced that it was carrying out tests to determine the cause of the infection. Initial tests ruled out leptospirosis and tuberculosis.

Colin Nicholas, executive director of the Centre for Orang Asli Concerns, told us that the root of the problem was the destruction of the natural habitat of the Bateq.

"The problem is not medical, but a direct result of what happens when people's rights to their customary lands are not recognised and that land is destroyed. Just seven to 10 years ago, if you visited them, they were perfectly healthy and psychologically happy. But their land has been taken away, in this case by the Kelantan state government. And their resource base has been destroyed."

The size disparity among Peninsular Malaysia's 18 Orang Asli tribes is wide. The largest tribe, the Semai, number more than 50,000. Tribes like the Jahai, Semaq Beri, Jah Hut, Mah Meri, Orang Seletar and Orang Kuala number less than 6,000, and the smallest, the Kensiu, Kintak, Lanoh, Mendriq, Che Wong and Orang Kanaq, all have less than 1,000 registered people per tribe. This means their language and culture may become extinct within a generation, which is what happened with the Kenaboi people. At the last census the Bateq, who are hunter-gatherers, numbered around 1,500 people.

Nicholas said that the villagers used to have a system that enabled them to live off the land. "At any one time, half the villagers would be hunting in the forest, and they would take turns. What has happened now is that without access to their traditional way of life, they have become malnourished and underweight. With their resistance being low, many diseases — whether it's pneumonia or tuberculosis, or even diarrhoea — can be fatal."

Nicholas' views were echoed by an outreach doctor Dr Steven Chow, who had visited the community on April 28, just a week before the deaths commenced.

"This is a community left behind, dying from neglect. After their land was taken away for plantations, these people were essentially left to fend on their own and were virtually cut off from the resources of the jungle which they had previously depended on for their survival."

Chow said he brought a medical team comprising volunteers, nurses, senior GPs (general practitioners) and dermatologists there in response to a call for help from another NGO following an article in the Malay press regarding a 'mysterious skin disease' afflicting many patients. Upon his arrival, Chow was deeply disturbed by what he saw.

"It was appalling. There was no running water. All the water tanks were empty. Pipes were broken. All we had was the bottled water that we brought along for the patients and the medical team. With no running water, the standard of sanitation was terrible. We saw patients from more than 60 families, many with multiple health problems. Almost all had infections affecting either the respiratory or gastrointestinal (systems), or the skin," Chow said.

The task confronting the team that descended on Kampung Kuala Koh was manifold. Healthy villagers were running away to avoid the deadly disease. In fact, it was reported that more than 150 Orang Asli from the Semaq Beri tribe had left their homes in Sungai Berua, Terengganu, because of an influx of Bateq villagers who had fled Kampung Kuala Koh. Of those who stayed back in Kampung Kuala Koh, some were very sick and needed to be taken to hospitals. Others were treated in the village itself, but the key issue was to determine the cause of the deaths of so many villagers.

Initial post-mortems indicated that two Bateq villagers had died of pneumonia, but an order was given for their bodies to be exhumed. Twelve more bodies had to be retrieved as they had been laid to rest according to traditional practice.

The traditional burial practice of the Bateq is for the corpse to be wrapped in tree bark and carried across a river, which according to their belief system, prevents the spirit from returning to the village. The body is then harnessed to a tall tree in the burial area using vines, and is left there to decompose. Burial grounds are considered taboo by the Bateq. Even though all of the dead were nominally Muslim, most still practised traditional ways.

Andrew recalled his visit there with sadness. "The first thing that struck me was the distance and the lack of basic facilities. Faza, an Orang Asli Semelai from Gombak, who was our driver, pointed out that the villages in the area are located close to the rivers for easy access to water as well as a means of transport and source of food supply. However, private companies encroaching into native lands to carry out commercial activities often destroyed their living environment and polluted the rivers that the Orang Asli depended on for survival.

"Along the drive from Kuala Lumpur cutting through Pahang and Kelantan, we saw several lorries entering into the jungle areas of the highways. The Department of Orang Asli Development (Jakoa) officer pointed out that the lorries could belong to developers looking for potential land for development. Upon reaching the Kampung Kuala Koh tragedy site, we were refused entry into the village as the General Operations Force and the police had cordoned off the entrance.

"At the operation command centre located nearby, there were many Bateq looking anxious and perplexed as they sought treatment and received food supplies from the Jakoa relief officers and other government agencies' staff. A doctor from the Gua Musang Hospital said the Orang Asli people often refused treatment as they depended on their traditional methods of healing but were forced to receive modern medicine treatment following the mysterious illness."

On June 14, Deputy Prime Minister Dr Wan Azizah Wan Ismail confirmed the Environment Department's findings that there was no water contamination from manganese mining at Aring 10, located three kilometres from Kampung Kuala Koh. Nonetheless, the human tragedy had exposed shortcomings in the administration of emergency medical treatment and raised questions about whether the destruction of the community's habitat or possible contamination of its water supply was behind the deaths.

The village headman (*tok batin*) Hamdan Keladi and three of his children were among the dead. His widow Som Ngai was in a daze over the loss of four family members in the space of two weeks. "I am still so sad, imagining the pain and suffering of my husband and children. I cannot do anything, even cooking and cleaning. I was so sorry to see their condition. Just lying and unable to eat or drink," she said.

Bateq toddler Nasri Rosli then became the 15th victim, passing away due to measles in a hospital in Kota Bharu. The Health Ministry also identified measles as the disease affecting the Bateq community. He said these cases were confirmed by laboratory tests, while the results for other diseases like tuberculosis, melioidosis, leptospirosis and coronavirus were negative.

Chow said that an outbreak of measles was a plausible explanation for the deaths, but attempts to link the community's way of life with the tragedy were not fair. He also dismissed the idea that the villagers were not keen to be vaccinated, and rejected claims that the nomadic lifestyle and burial practices of the Bateq might have played a role in the deaths.

On June 29, Jakoa Director-General Juli Edo told a forum that when he visited the stricken Bateq village, "there was clearly a divide, a 'them and us' situation, and the relationship between the government service providers and the villagers was not warm".

He went on to admit that 'the majority' of Jakoa staff were 'not passionate' about their work, and were there just to '*makan gaji*' (earn a salary). He also lamented the 'ethnocentric attitude' of the staff, noting that in Kelantan, the authorities seemed more keen to convert the Orang Asli to Islam rather than improve their living standards.

Juli warned that more deaths could be expected if the poverty of the Orang Asli was not addressed. "The Orang Asli community is still mired in poverty, with nearly 99 percent of them belonging to the B40 income group and most of them in the hardcore poor category. What happened in Kuala Koh is a lesson to all. In order to prevent this tragedy from recurring, the first step is for the government to strive to alleviate the Orang Asli community from poverty."

On July 6, the Health Ministry said that laboratory testing of three of the dead Orang Asli from Kuala Koh, Gua Musang, confirmed that the cause of death was complications due to measles. However, the post-mortems carried out on the other 12 bodies found by the police could not determine the cause of death, largely due to decomposition and contamination. These 12 bodies were the ones originally buried according to traditional Bateq rites.

A day later, Gua Musang Police Chief Mohd Taufik Maidin said the district disaster committee had decided to lift the red zone restriction effective from 8am, July 8, after the area was confirmed to be safe from any infectious diseases.

On July 18, fresh doubts on the underlying cause of the deaths emerged when laboratory tests on samples taken from the waters sourced around Kampung Kuala Koh revealed contamination and toxic substances.

Chow told us the samples were taken on June 10 and 11 from five sources and sent for testing in three independent laboratories.

The results of these tests revealed that samples from Sungai Pertang — the main source of water for the community — were not suitable for human consumption unless extensively treated. The water is not even suitable for recreational use.

The Health Ministry is still looking into the case at the time of publication, but life, for the likes of Som Ngai and many others, will never be the same again.

VERDICT The mystery illness, so commonplace in urban centres, wreaked havoc on a community that has been marginalised and disconnected.

ABOUT THE AUTHORS

 MARTIN VENGADESAN is part of Malaysiakini's editorial team. He previously worked at *The Star* from 1996 to 2018. He specialises in historical and research-based articles and also spent many years in the digital section as editor of *The Star*'s iPad app and popular news website *The Star Online*. He wrote two columns for *The Star*, 'Music Myths & Legends' (2002-2012) and 'Watching The World' (2013-2018) which touched on music history and world politics respectively. He contributed chapters to the best-selling *March 8: The Day Malaysia Woke Up* and the *KL Noir* series. He has served as general treasurer of the National Union of Journalists and was formerly general secretary of the Youth Wing of Parti Rakyat Malaysia and a vice-president of the Youth Wing of Parti Keadilan Rakyat. A father of three, he is the son of former diplomat Ambassador R Vengadesan.

 ANDREW SAGAYAM is part of Malaysiakini's editorial team. He was formerly press secretary in the Prime Minister's Deparment. He was also a crime reporter, news editor and TV producer between 1998 and 2019 with *The Sun, Malay Mail, The Star* and *Bernama*. He has covered many of the most prominent cases of the last two decades, giving him an insight few others enjoy.

In the early 1980s, the pair attended the same primary school (Sekolah Sri Petaling) and church (St Francis Xavier) without having met. This changed in 1996 when they briefly played in a band together. Formerly recording artistes (with Samarkand and Bent Wavelength respectively), they joined forces to record as Martin Vengadesan & The Stalemate Factor, which has released three CDs in the past three years — *The Queen's Gambit, The Bishop's Sacrifice* and *The Knight's Flight*. A fourth CD called *The Rook's Siege* is on the way. Any crimes the duo may have committed have not been included in this anthology.

Research sources include *The Star,*
New Straits Times, Malay Mail,
The Straits Times (Singapore),
The Malaysian Bar, as well as credited
books and documentaries.